CHINA TRAVAIL

The Story of William Englund

WILLIAM H. PAPE

133 2

The Evangelical Alliance Mission
Wheaton, Illinois 60187

Published by The Evangelical Alliance Mission
Wheaton, Ilinois 60187

Library of Congress Catalog Card Number: 75-30149
ISBN: 0-916248-00-3

Note on style: The author has endeavored to uniformly transliterate Chinese proper names as follows: first name capitalized; second and third names joined by a hyphen, with only the first of the two being capitalized.

Foreword

How do you determine greatness in a man? Is it measured by public notice or acclaim? Is it related to the monument of a great institution he founded with his name over the door? Is it a certain mystic charisma that has made him a favorite of thousands?

The subject of this book, William Gideon Englund, had true greatness. It did not come to wide public notice nor was it the result of any institution which bears his name. There was a winsomeness or charisma, it is true, but it had to bear the burden of deafness and so could not find its true expression.

Dr. Englund's greatness was of spiritual dimension — in devotion, faith, fellowship with God and great concern for his fellow men, saved and unsaved alike.

There is actually a monument to his greatness. It is the church in Northwest China. I use the present tense because I do not believe the church has been destroyed. Buffeted and beleaguered as they may be, God's own people are surely there. "The Lord knoweth them that are His."

William Pape, who himself served in China, has captured the essence of Dr. Englund's ministry and the secret of its fruitfulness. I have read his manuscript with unusual interest for more than one reason. Dr. Englund was a fellow TEAM missionary and Mrs. Mortenson and I had the added personal privilege of serving on the field with William and Anna Englund. There we witnessed true missionary greatness being forged on the anvil of daily pressure, during years of war and economic upheaval when open doors of opportunity were diligently entered.

Vernon Mortenson
General Director
The Evangelical Alliance Mission

Contents

1

Identification

Laughing, sweating coolies dragged ropes over the Shanghai dock to the capstans. The SS Empress of Asia was completing another trans-pacific crossing. Looking at the ship's log, the first mate remarked (to no one in particular) that 19 days was not bad, considering the weather.

Shanghai was symbolic of violent changes shaking the ancient foundations of the Middle Kingdom. Part of the city was entirely under foreign control; its International Settlement not subject to Chinese law. Sikh policemen directed people and traffic. The collection of customs dues at all treaty ports was in the hands of a foreign staff under a British Inspector General. Russia had built a naval base at Port Arthur on the Liaotung peninsula. Germany had done the same at Tsingtao in Shantung province. And France, in addition to a naval base in South China, had a concession to build a railroad from Indochina to Kunming, capital of Yunnan province.

Other pressures were threatening old structures. For nearly ten years Dr. Sun Yat-sen had been enlisting support to overthrow the ruling Manchus. The classical examination system, for 19 centuries the basis of Chinese education and society, was being criticized by progressive Mandarins. China was preparing to swallow the bitter pill of Western learning.

Chiang Kai-shek, finishing his civil schooling, was turning his eyes toward a military career. And on a farm in Hunan, Mao Tse-tung, tall and strong, was planting rice, gathering scarce firewood, and sullenly carrying great baskets of manure on his father's farm. Revolution was in the air.

In Peking, the Dowager Empress, Tsu Hsi, schemed and fought to buttress her crumbling Manchu dynasty against Chinese revolutionary movements and Western imperialism. A gesture of her jeweled hand determined the fate of thousands, while the young Emperor sat in fading splendor on the Dragon Throne with little understanding and no control over the turbulent events swirling around him. Known in Court circles as "Old Buddha," the Empress had approved the extermination of all foreigners in China by "The Harmonious Fists" Society, better known as the terrible "Boxers." The allied guns of six nations had brought the massacre to an end. Christians of any nationality had been the special object of Boxer hatred, and 200 missionaries had been murdered. But more foreigners were coming, including William Gideon Englund, who stepped ashore with his bride, Lena. The date was September 26, 1903. They had been married only eight weeks. The bridegroom had grown a beard with the dual purpose of compensating for the age difference between himself and his wife, and of hiding his youth from Chinese eyes. The strategy was so effective that a woman who heard him speak before leaving for China asked him, when she saw him again on furlough without the beard, if he had ever met the "old Mr. Englund?"

For Lena, the sights of Shanghai were not new. She had already served one term of a remarkable career. Furlough had been beyond her highest hopes. In her native Sweden, God had used her to bring revival wherever she spoke, and had given her a unique opportunity to preach in a State church, which normally denied women their pulpit. And in Minnesota, where she saw revival come to many Scandinavian congregations, she met William Englund. Drawn together by a passionate desire to lead people of all ages to a personal knowledge of Christ, and with a common interest in taking the gospel to China, they were happily married and ready for the joys and hazards of missionary service.

The impact of Western culture on old China was neither as sudden nor dramatic as the impact of China on William Englund and his fellow missionaries. Identification with the people they had come to serve was without limit. In the early 1900's occidental and oriental styles were radically different. Long sleeved, voluminous jackets of rather ambiguous shape, and baggy pants, often bound at the ankles with cotton leggings in the cold north, seemed designed to hide the fact that anyone was inside. Englund thoughtfully surveyed the strange garments. He had always been immaculate and would never be careless of his appearance, but without hesitation he exchanged his American suit for the Chinese clothes. His motive was clear and deliberate. He was not collecting a native costume to add color to a missionary rally on furlough, but breaking down a barrier between himself and the people he had come to serve. He looked in the mirror. Very little of William Englund was visible. His hands had disappeared in the long sleeves. His body had no particular shape. Only his head was recognizable. And identification with the Chinese demanded an exacting change there. For generations young men have had strong opinions about hair styles; crew cut, medium or long, and conformity to the norm is part of their way of life. To wear the clothes of another nation might even be romantic, but for a bridegroom of 21 to have his head as clean-shaven as an egg could be traumatic. Manchu law required every Chinese to grow a pigtail as an outward sign of servility. But until nature took its course, Englund could conform only by pinning an artificial queue to the little round hat which he placed on his sheared head. Another look in the mirror satisfied him the transformation was complete. In outward appearance, William Gideon Englund had become a Chinese. He was no longer to be identified primarily with the diplomats, soldiers, merchants and adventurers of Western nations and their secular interests, so different, and at times in conflict with those of the Christian missionary. Even his Swedish family name, and names prayerfully given him by loving parents were surrendered for Christ and China's sake. He was now I En-cheng, the only name by which he would be known to thousands of Chinese. Englund's eyes began to twinkle as he looked at his reflection. And then he laughed. He had passed the first of two tests he later used to assess new missionaries. "He must have a good sense of humor and no sense of smell," he asserted. Englund's companion took her turn looking in the mirror, and burst into tears.

Clothes, hair and name had all become Chinese, but these were outward changes. Inner adjustments were needed, more difficult and slower to achieve.

China already had more than 4,000 years of history in which religion and philosophy had harmoniously matured. Deep rooted culture had elevated the nation to a peak from which all others seemed to be barbarians. China was the "Middle Kingdom;" other races were the "outsiders." Symbolic of their ancient culture, and an essential part of it, was the Chinese language, elegant and artistic when written, musical when spoken; a single character often expressing a complete philosophic truth. To master the language and understand the philosophy of China was Englund's first task.

He had several special advantages, not the least being a wife who had already become fluent in Chinese. He also had unusual language ability. As a little child he had absorbed Swedish from his parents in Minnesota. This he never confused with Norwegian picked up from neighbors. At school he had learned English, and when he sailed for China he was fluent and able to preach in all three languages. In addition, Englund had the precious gifts of a retentive memory and a musical ear.

William and Lena Englund turned their backs on the International Settlement in Shanghai and set out for Sian in Shensi province. The distance is about 650 miles, as the crow flies, but people then were not able to follow the example of that excellent bird. The mighty Yangtze River was the easiest way to Hankow. From there travelers enjoyed the relative tranquility of a Han River boat before transferring to mule litters for the balance of the journey. Slung in a hammock-like contraption secured to two beasts of capricious temperament and uncertain cooperation, Englund had plenty of leisure to meditate on what might be ahead. What his own imagination lacked was supplied by other travelers in wild tales of hairbreadth escapes from robbers related over spluttering oil lamps in the inns where they took lodging each night. Such experiences were to become routine, but he was glad when the high, broad walls of Sian eventually broke the monotony of the otherwise uninterrupted dusty horizon. Two months was a long time for so short a journey, and well illustrated the old Chinese proverb, "Don't worry about going slowly, only fear coming to a complete stop." Truly the days had not been wasted. By prayer, study and with considerable help from Lena, Englund had gone through a primer printed by the China Inland Mission and had become familiar with some of the basics of Chinese. He was ready for a study in depth of that fascinating language.

Shensi province is the cradle of the Chinese race. Sian, its capital, was founded in the 12th century before Christ. For 300 years, ending in 915 A.D., it was the capital of the great Tang dynasty. During that period Nestorian missionaries from Syria brought the gospel to China, and founded churches which survived for several centuries. Marco Polo, the Venetian merchant who traveled to "Cathay," as China was known in the 13th century, found Christian congregations along the route of his historic journey. But those churches died out through compromise with native myths and philosophy, and North China had to wait another 600 years before the gospel was brought to them in pure form. Itinerant missionaries of the China Inland Mission were the first to reach Shensi province, followed by pioneers of the Scandinavian Alliance Mission*, who arrived in 1891.

After a brief stop in Sian, William and Lena Englund settled in the village of Chenchiakou, Lantien County, a day's cart journey from Sian. Identification with the Chinese entered a new phase as they settled into a typical local house of mud bricks and mud floor, partly covered with reed mats. The bed was a "kang," made of brick and with a built-in fireplace so that it could be heated in the bitterly cold winters. Snug crevices between warm bricks appealed to many a poisonous scorpion looking for winter quarters, and when spring came Englund was alarmed to find that he had not had sole occupancy of the bed. In daytime, the house was heated by an open pan of glowing

---

*By 1949 members of the Mission were no longer predominantly Scandinavian and the name was changed to The Evangelical Alliance Mission, or TEAM. To avoid confusion, the new name will be used throughout this book.

charcoal, of which the poisonous fumes were almost as lethal as the sting of scorpions.

The Chinese language was quite different from anything Englund had ever studied. The majority of words are of one syllable, and each word is represented by a single character which may have as many as 28 strokes, each to be written in the correct order and style. There is no alternative to memorizing by sight. In the introduction to his famous Chinese-English dictionary, R. H. Matthews, of the China Inland Mission (now the Overseas Missionary Fellowship) says, "The number of Chinese characters included in this book has been increased to 7,785 . . . this selection of characters should meet the need of the average student." Many a young missionary struggling to be average would gladly have settled for less. And one desperate student, wearily working on the massive task of translating a Chinese book into English, wondered whether his thumb or the dictionary would wear out first.

In the little village of Chenchiakou, Englund followed the traditional method of study. The classics were an important part of the curriculum for Chinese day school students, many of whom learned the whole lesson by heart. Englund did the same, listening carefully as his teacher read rhythmic phrases from the great scholars of ancient China, Confucius ranking as the chief. His quick ear began to distinguish between similar sounds spoken in a different pitch or *tone*. This was important, because one of the difficulties of the Chinese spoken language is that most sounds can be pronounced in three, or even four tones, each having an entirely different meaning. *Chu*, for example, can mean, *a lord*, and often *the Lord*; or *a pillar*, or a *pig*, according to the tone in which it is pronounced. Fortified with sips of tea, the teacher loudly recited the ancient phrases, emphasizing their cadences with rhythmic movements of his body. Englund echoed each sentence of the teacher, sometimes having to repeat the same word time and time again until the pronunciation was satisfactory. The only interruption came when the teacher would point with his little finger to a particular character and exclaim, "This word truly is full of meaning. In a lifetime one could not fully expound it." Chinese language and learning was becoming embedded in Englund's mind, and when his first test came he was ready. Following the custom of Chinese students, Englund sat with his back to the teacher and repeated from memory the complete book which they had been studying together, and the old scholar, listening meticulously, nearly forgot that his pupil was a foreigner. In identifying with the Chinese people, Englund acquired a characteristic which he never lost. Through constant contact with his teacher and people of the village, he acquired the distinctive accent of Lantien city. Later, when he began to travel extensively through Shensi province to speak at Bible conferences, his request to the congregation to turn to the first chapter of Ephesians often brought forth a smile, and someone was sure to turn to his neighbor and whisper, "You hear how Pastor I* pronounces *Ephesians*? He is from Lantien!"

In the early 1900's the strong antiforeign movement, which had come to a terrible climax with the Boxer massacre, had not died out. William Englund soon found that it was easier to identify with the people than to be accepted by them. He was following in the footsteps of his Master, who "came unto his own and his own received him not . . ."

February, 1904 was the time of the Chinese Spring Festival. Englund had been in China only four months, but had already completed the first six sections of language study, which usually took a year. The village streets were packed as crowds celebrated with feasts, processions and plays. Englund's teacher advised him to secure all the doors, and stay at home. But shortly, the rattle of stones and the thud of bricks thrown down on the roof from a hill at the back of the house were a sharp warning that violence was planned. Soon a noisy crowd was pushing at the door, trying to break in. Englund turned to his wife, "They seem to be looking for us," he shouted above the din, "I'll get my mandolin, and go out and see if I can draw them away from here." Englund was a little man, but when he opened the door and stepped out, he was accompanied by God, his Father almighty. He looked at the angry, hostile faces. Shaking back the long sleeves of his Chinese gown, he firmly grasped the mandolin and struck a few chords. It sounded no more than the twittering of a bird in a tempest. Then with a prayer in his heart and a song on his lips, he began playing a Chinese melody. He had a good and powerful voice, and as he sang, he moved slowly away from the house to a small rise on the other side of a gulley. The people followed, their anger giving way to amazement that a foreigner could sing in their language and play their tunes. Englund continued until he knew no more, and then used his limited Chinese vocabulary to preach at the impromptu open-air service.

God miraculously turned a dangerous situation into a golden opportunity. Like Peter at Pentecost, Englund had no time to prepare a special message for the occasion but God had prepared His servant. Long hours of prayer, and Bible study, and many days of patient perseverance at his Chinese books had born fruit. The crowd dispersed, discussing music and message. Englund smiled a farewell, talked to one or two who lingered, and then slowly walked back to his home where Lena welcomed him with thanksgiving.

"I never stopped praying for you, not even for one minute," she said. Englund sat down. He was tired. What a day it had been! Barriers between East and West had been broken down. Chinese clothes,

---

*pronounced ē

hat and queue had helped. A working knowledge of the language had made communication possible. Chinese melodies had touched angry hearts. And God by His Spirit had spoken through William Englund to a people without God, without Christ and without hope.

2

Pioneer

The word *pioneer* carries a hint of glamor which reality often fails to provide. The original French meaning of *foot soldier* is nearer to the truth. William Englund was indeed a soldier of Jesus Christ. All his long life each day began with physical exercises done with military precision. And his ministry in China began with a penetration of new areas with the gospel. He established beachheads for Christ in areas that were spiritually hostile. Prayer often accompanied by fasting and the Word of God were his weapons. A powerful voice and an irrepressible sense of humor were supporting gifts.

In the early 1900's China was in no way eagerly pleading for the Church to *"send the light."* Missionaries walking the streets were more likely to hear loud references to *"foreign devils."* Adopting Chinese customs, clothes and language, did not completely remove the suspicion that the teachers of the *"Christ Religion"* were part of a sinister plan to plunder China. Pioneers were especially subject to smoldering hatred, which often broke out into violence. When weeks of hot sun and rainless days parched the fields and famine threatened, villagers thronged to the local temple to pray to their gods. Continuing drought made the people reinforce their prayers with fasting. But no rain came. No one dared to suggest that the gods were indifferent, and obviously prayer, incense and fasting was all that could reasonably be expected of even the most devout. Suspicion instinctively turned towards the local missionaries, and a few inquiries soon revealed that they were eating meat and eggs as usual. The word spread through the village like a raging fire, and resentment of the foreign intruders increased. The Englunds decided on the diplomatic course of eliminating eggs and meat from their diet. But rumor and exaggeration supplied what was lacking in fact, and hostility grew worse. In time of drought Elijah the prophet had once dramatically proved through prayer that Jehovah alone is God. Englund decided to do the same. With his wife and a few Christian Chinese he began a full day of fasting and prayer. People passing the house heard strong pleadings to the God of heaven and earth, and looked up at the shimmering blue sky to see if the Lord of the Christians was more powerful than their own gods. Hour followed hour; the streets still dry and dusty. And with more weariness than triumph, thirsty villagers muttered to each other, "Their God also does not hear." But by evening Englund's prayers turned to praise. Heavy clouds came rushing across the sky. The hot sun blotted out before it reached the horizon. Showers became a downpour so abundant that the parched earth could not gulp it down fast enough, and raindrops splashing into puddles danced with exhuberant joy to the glory of God.

William Englund was a little man with a big voice, clear and strong. Microphones and amplifiers had not then appeared to transform whispers into roars, but Englund needed no artificial helps. He had no difficulty in making himself heard to a congregation of a thousand or more people. The quality of his voice always amazed doctors. It was inconsistent with a tuberculosis history. Englund himself had felt that three insuperable obstacles stood in the way of the missionary career suggested to him by Solomon Bergstrom, home from China because of the Boxer uprising. He had TB of the lungs; he lacked adequate training and he had no financial support. But God distilled all three arguments into one critical issue. Would William Englund yield himself unconditionally to God's will or not. The crisis came. He looked up as if into the face of God, and cried out, "O Lord, I here and now completely yield myself to Thee. Let Thy will be done, and I will not hold back on any point." But tuberculosis was still a fact and Englund and Lena decided on a day of fasting and prayer. Beginning early in the morning, their prayers mingled and they became more and more conscious of God's presence. Englund, already sure that he was to go to China, boldly reminded the Lord that strong lungs would be needed for pioneer evangelism and a life of preaching, and then surrendered what he had. "I give over my weak lungs to you, dear Lord," he prayed, and from that time on the tuberculosis was gone. Physical examinations later showed only scars on the lungs. Tiredness would come, but through all of 70 strenuous years of preaching on the China Mainland, Taiwan, Hong Kong, Japan, Norway, Sweden and the United States, he was never handicapped by his lungs failing or his voice becoming hoarse. God had decided that His servant was well qualified for the rugged life of a missionary.

Englund's first center for evangelism was the city of Lantien, about ten miles from the village where he had begun language study. He and Lena moved there in 1906. His first task was to repair the house and build a chapel. Carpentry was nothing new to him. His father had been born on Aland Island, belonging to Finland, but inhabited by Swedes. When the family immigrated to America, settling in Minnesota, Gustave Englund had built his own log cabin. William, growing up under primitive conditions, gained plenty of experience with hammer and saw, which now proved useful in Lantien. Incomplete language study took a new turn. A sedate and dignified hour or two with a teacher of classics was replaced by interminable haggling over the price of lumber in the market place.

The Lantien church had been born in suffering. The first to believe was a Moslem who was officially punished with fifty lashes for his faith in Christ. The Boxer uprising of 1900 had brought the work to a standstill, and when Englund began his ministry, there were only 15 members. In all directions were numerous villages with thousands of people lost in the dull routine of a purposeless existence. The new chapel was built opposite the main Taoist temple of the city. The Religion of the Way or "Tao" had its origin centuries before the birth of Christ, but a quest after peace of heart, which the harmonious universe eternally proclaimed, had proved elusive. One of the Taoist priests was fascinated by the faces of the little congregation attending the chapel. He determined to find the answer to a persistant question which tormented him. He crossed the street to talk with an elderly Chinese Christian. "Old Sir, you seem to have a special peace when you come out of this place," he said. "This is what I'm seeking. I gave up my home to become a priest. I have been in some of our great temples without finding what my heart longs for. What is it that gives you such peace? And you all seem to have such joy and fellowship when you meet. What is the secret of that?" When told that peace and salvation are from Jesus Christ, the priest replied, "If He can give such peace as that, then I want your Jesus too." He began to attend the small street chapel, adjoining the main church building and bought Gospels and Christian literature to study.

At dawn on Chinese New Year's day, Englund had a visitor who was vaguely familiar. The man smiled. "Don't you recognize me?," he said. "I'm the priest who used to be in the temple opposite. But I have turned to Christ, and today left the temple forever. I have found what I was looking for, and now I'm going back home." He had cut off his long hair, and changed his Taoist robes for ordinary clothes. As a token of his thankfulness to God, he had a gift for Englund, and in preparation for the journey, bought a New Testament so that he could witness to Christ along the way.

Pioneer evangelism in northwest China often followed the turbulent pattern vividly described in the Acts of the Apostles. About 20 miles from Lantien was a large market town set on a hill. Two Chinese Christians had opened a house of refuge there for any who wanted help in breaking off the terrible opium smoking habit. They sent an invitation to William and Lena Englund to bring the gospel to the town which was notorious as a hideout for robbers, gamblers and opium smokers. Thankful for such an opportunity, the Englunds accepted. At the foot of the hill, as they neared the town, they saw a tremendous crowd gathered for a theatrical performance in honor of the local gods. Uncertain of the people's reaction to the sight of the foreigner, Englund asked one of his Chinese fellow workers to contact the local officials, and explain to them the purpose of his visit. When the message was ignored, he decided to enter the town by a small path which circled the hill. But the crowd caught sight of them, and rushed in hot pursuit, shouting bloodcurdling threats at the "foreign devils." By the time the pioneer evangelists reached the main street, threats had given way to stones, hurled at them with equal fury. Up went missionary umbrellas as protection against the barrage, leaving only the imperturbable horses vulnerable to the attack. The opium refuge was a small building, but when Englund and his party entered, the entire crowd tried to follow. Those who could not shove their way through the door climbed in at the windows. The situation was so dangerous that Englund began to wonder if his missionary career was about to come to an early end. But during the noise and turmoil, he turned instinctively to God. "My heart looked to the Lord, and we experienced His presence," he said, when telling the story years later.

God responded immediately. The day had been cloudless, but suddenly the sky turned dark, thunder roared angrily and terrifying flashes of lightning stabbed the earth. Then rain fell as if another flood were about to destroy the world. People who had forced their way into the house tried to rush out only to meet a crowd of equal size trying to get in. When the incredible confusion died down, only the Christians remained.

The rain continued without a break for three days. The theatricals which were planned to honor China's traditional gods were literally washed out but the preaching of the gospel was accomplished in peace and quietness to an attentive audience.

News of the town's hostile reception of Englund reached the ears of the Lantien magistrate who was enraged that such discourtesy had been shown to his friend. He summoned the officials to his office, intending to punish them severely for failing to protect the visiting preachers. But at Englund's special request, the magistrate limited his action to a stern lecture in which he informed the culprits that, but for the kindheartedness of the missionary, they would all have been in serious trouble. In an effort to restore themselves to the magistrate's favor, the town authorities sent a deputation of five leading men to apologize to Englund, and made further recompense for their misdeeds by providing him with a much better house to stay in on his second visit.

The pioneer effort, with all its dangers, was not in vain. Men and women were delivered from the power of darkness and a futile faith in nonexistent gods. Englund looked at the little company of new believers and thanked God. Much teaching and training was needed. Some in the group could not read. No one had any knowledge of the Bible, or of the privileges and responsibilities of a child of God. But a church had been born. Their meeting place was an old store building converted into a simple chapel, with a second floor as sleeping quarters for visitors coming from a distance. At the end of a long day of preaching, teaching and counseling, Englund and his companion settled down in these quarters for the night. That was the signal for a multitude of bedbugs to start operations. They came from everywhere; bed frame, walls and ceiling. Sleep was absolutely impossible. The following day at Englund's request, the beds were replaced by benches and boards. But potent aerosol sprays did not then exist to wipe out irritating insects, and nothing could be done to eliminate countless enemies lurking in every crack in the walls and ceiling. As night came around, Englund knelt wearily beside his bed to pray, and into his mind came the story of God's angels smiting the men of Sodom with blindness so that they could not find the door of Lot's house. "Lord," he prayed, "we feel so tired, and need sleep so badly, but with all these insects it's impossible. We know that they will soon be able to find these new beds prepared for us, but if You could smite the Sodomites with blindness so that they couldn't find the door of Lot's house, then You can smite these bedbugs with blindness so that they can't find our bed." Englund laughed as he told the story, and concluded, "We were there several days and not one bedbug found us!"

Ten miles from the new little church was another town where two men resided who had been converted and delivered from slavery to opium at the House of Refuge. When they heard that Englund was in the area, they sent a message urging him to spend at least three days in their town. Englund and his Chinese fellow workers decided to accept the call for another pioneer effort. Their reception could not have been more encouraging. The crowd which gathered in the main street was so enormous that Englund and one of the Chinese preachers separated to different parts of the town, each drawing hundreds of eager listeners with him. For two whole days the town gave careful attention to God's good news of a Savior sent from Heaven for man's salvation. Englund especially noticed an old man listening intently and, after he finished preaching, was delighted to be invited to visit him. The old man took Englund to his store, which contained a little shrine. "These are my gods which I have faithfully worshipped daily," he explained, "but now I have decided that I will trust Jesus Christ for salvation. Please arrange a suitable ceremony." He threw out the shrine, burnt the wood and paper gods and pondered what to do with a special Buddha made of brass. Children playing in the street gave him an idea. Throwing it to them with a laugh, he said that they could have it as a toy, and with a prayer to the living God, Englund committed the new believer and his store to Christ.

Torrential rain which had dispersed a hostile crowd on Englund's first pioneer trip now threatened the friendly enthusiasm shown on his second effort. Prayer that had been effective in bringing rain now failed to stop it. But God had a better plan in mind. Two large homes were offered as meeting places for those who wanted to hear more about Christ. For two weeks neither the rain nor the home gatherings stopped. Day by day people splashed their way along muddy streets. Women, handicapped by their tiny bound feet, were carried on the backs of their husbands. The town was hungry for the gospel. No less than 22 complete families voluntarily threw away their idols and turned to Christ. The house in which Englund stayed was made available for regular services until a more adequate building could be erected.

As the two wonderful weeks came to an end, rain was still pouring down. Tired after an unusually busy day, Englund prepared for a well-earned rest. His bed was in a corner of the room right behind a large coffin, which he presumed to be empty. Without asking, no one could be sure. It might have been a casket bought in readiness for the sad day when it would be needed, or it might have been a full casket being kept for a lucky burial day. As he lay down to rest, the rain pounded on the roof and began finding its way through the tiles. No matter where Englund moved his bed, he could not escape the steady drips. His umbrella which had shielded him from stones in a hostile town now reverted to its original purpose as he opened it up to keep part of himself and the bed dry. But sleep still eluded him. It was not thoughts of death prompted by the casket which kept him awake, nor a leaky roof and wet bedding but a heart overflowing with joy at what God had done in the hearts of so many. Who would not be a pioneer for God when even the earthly rewards are so great?

3

Revival

Our Lord's command to preach the gospel in all the world was coupled with a promise of His continual presence, implying that the mission would be accomplished by supernatural means. William Englund was deeply convinced of this. He knew that China would not be won to Christ merely by wearing Chinese clothes, growing a queue, mastering the difficult language and witnessing to the people by word and life. He and other missionaries had seen small churches established, but the sight of noisy crowds thronging the market place or following an idol procession was a terrible reminder that the great majority were still without Christ. The early years of pioneer evangelism had been like an angler with rod and line using all his skill to catch one fish from a reluctant shoal. A net was needed.

Remembering what God had done in his native Minnesota, Englund began to pray for revival. In his own words, "the burden of it weighed so heavily upon me that I just felt that I didn't want to do anything else, only give myself to pray." He had every reason to believe that God would answer. From the time of the great Welsh revival, there had been a kind of jet stream of mighty power circling the earth. In 1901, God used a farmer by the name of Tunheim to bring revival to the Minnesota Red River Valley. Two years later Korea experienced the irresistible wind of God sweeping through their churches, and coinciding with a visit by Fredrik Franson. In Manchuria, God had spoken through Jonathan Goforth, demonstrating that revival is "not by might, nor by power but by my Spirit, saith the Lord of hosts . . ." Also in 1908, Albert Lutley, of the China Inland Mission, who had been with Goforth, visited Sian City in Shensi province with his associate Mr. Wang, and revival came to the great Northwest.

The impact of God's presence was devastating. Any who expected revival to be a time of enthusiastic singing and joyful excitement were quickly disillusioned. People whose commitment to Christ was nominal were so convicted of sin that they were brokenhearted and wept until the floor of the church was wet for days. Others, filled with remorse, banged their heads against the wooden pillars of the church, or smote their breasts in desperate contrition. Yet others fainted, remaining unconscious for long periods, and then found relief as, with open eyes, they poured out their confession to God. The Spirit of God forced Christians to admit what torture could not have dragged from their lips. Such sins as stealing, lying, dishonesty in money matters, and even contemplating or committing murder were confessed before the whole church. The revival for which Englund had been praying had come.

One of those attending a small church near Lantien was a farmer who, although a Christian, continued secretly to grow and sell opium. He suddenly stood in one of the services. "In my store I have a large supply of opium on which I planned to make a big profit," he said. "Now God has shown me my sin. Will one of the brothers please come and help me get rid of it?" A Chinese elder offered to help, and the two men immediately left the church. Together they took the great lump of opium and set fire to it in the street. Its sickly sweet odor brought people from all directions to see what was happening. The opium smokers were especially shocked. "This is a terrible thing," they said; "Think how much money is going up in smoke. That opium would have kept us going for months." At that, the farmer jumped up on a large stone in the street to tell what God had done for him. Some who heard were furious, and his wife criticized him bitterly. But from that day on, the farmer was a new man. Although never much of a speaker, he was always ready to witness for his Lord. One of the first to turn to Christ through his revived testimony was his repenting wife.

When asked to detail revival characteristics, Englund listed seven. First was an intensely deep conviction of sin. Christians who had thought of sin only as loss to themselves or injury to others were horrified at the ugliness of their transgressions in the sight of a holy God. Sometimes even before the preacher had read his text, a great wave of conviction would smite the congregation and for hours contrite believers would stand, one after another, to make confession. To them all, the Cross became more precious than ever as they sought fresh cleansing from the Redeemer.

Secondly, revival was a spiritual housecleaning. Stolen property was restored. To some it proved costly, as an elder of the Lantien church discovered. Listening to Englund preaching, he was convicted by God's Spirit of taking church money for his personal use. A rather stiff and stubborn man, he was the first to stand and confess his dishonesty with tears. He repaid the money, and a year later testified that God had so wonderfully blessed him that he had decided to increase his tithe to a fifth of all he received. He kept his promise to the end of his life and his harsh, unrelenting attitude gave way to a sympathetic tenderness towards everyone.

A third consequence of revival was a new spiritual atmosphere in the churches. Englund wrote, "Before it came, some hearts felt greatly burdened, and there were continual wrestlings in prayer until the fire fell. What a melting of hearts it caused! Up until that time the power of the gospel had been manifested in bringing souls from darkness to light, and from the power of Satan unto God, and in the establishing of churches, yet there was a lack of deeper heart stirrings. But when the fire of the Holy Spirit struck, even strong men of the proudest nature broke down before the Lord, and sometimes in meetings the sound of weeping could be heard far out on the street. I remember a man whose haughty and unyielding temper was well known. After his pride had been broken he said in a testimony that the meetings had been a great blessing to his heart, but mighty hard on his face. The Spirit's work is not face-saving."

A fourth characteristic of revival was unity among Christians. Hearts melted toward God were melted toward each other. Ill feeling, friction, hatred, bitterness and enmity were confessed and cleansed. God's people began to demonstrate the sweet unity for which Christ Himself prayed.

Fifthly, revival brought a new desire to pray. Traditional phrases and old clichés were forgotten as people brought their praises and petitions to God in fresh, spontaneous language inspired by the Holy Spirit. Fervency, earnestness and openness marked the prayer meetings, giving new momentum to the church's development and outreach.

A sixth consequence of revival was an increase in giving. Christians became less materialistic. Women gladly gave their jewels and silver ornaments to the Lord, and men were as willing to give their time as well as their money for God's service. Those who had least, gave all they could. In one service, many expressed their thankfulness to God for new blessings by making generous offerings and pledges, but a young evangelist had nothing to offer. He had come in from the country and spent all his meager savings on a splendid white summer suit which he had seen in a city store. He suddenly stood up and walked to Englund at the front of the church. "Pastor I," he said, "I still have my old suit, and I'll get along with that. Take this new suit, sell it for whatever you can get, and use the money for the Lord's work." He became a wonderful servant of God, and a channel of revival blessing through all his district.

The seventh characteristic which Englund observed in revival was a new passion to win people for Jesus Christ. Many Christians pledged part of their time to go out to towns and villages to witness. Gospel bands were formed for itinerant evangelism. Hearts were aflame with love for God and a burning desire to make Christ known. Even the poorest and humblest believer found that he could be used to lead others into the faith.

Englund met such a man one day when preaching in a small chapel. A ragged coolie walked in and, setting his bamboo carrying pole and loads just inside the door, took a seat. Englund, who often punctuated his preaching with questions to the audience, was amazed that the coolie knew all the answers. After the service, he talked with the man and found that he made a living by buying odds and ends, such as used nails and cans in one village, and selling them in the next. "But can you make a living that way?" asked Englund. "Of course," the coolie answered with a laugh. "The Lord meets my needs. I'm not traveling around to make money but to tell people about Jesus Christ." Out of curiosity Englund asked God's ragged salesman if he sang as well as witnessed. "I don't really have a singing voice," he replied, "but I do know a few hymns." And pulling a steel triangle from one of his baskets, he held it up by a string and tapped out the time with a long iron nail as he sang huskily "Bringing in the sheaves." He had only one eye, but as he reached the line, "We shall reap in that Heavenly home," he looked up as if anticipating the happy day when he would see his Savior. Then he shouldered his loads, and went his way.

The church revived became the church triumphant. When Christians were right with God, unbelievers were brought to Christ. Many who heard of the great revival feared and said, "The Christian's God has come among them." One visitor attending the evening services stepped forward at the close and said, "I have never been in contact with the Christian religion and know nothing about it, but what I have seen and heard here has convinced me that this is the work of the living God." The spiritual breakthrough, for which so many had prayed and worked, had come. The churches were no longer an insignificant minority but centers where God's mighty power was being demonstrated. The impact of revival was to be felt for at least two decades.

Englund personally was convinced that persistent, fervent prayer would always bring revival. A Chinese Christian who knew him well said, "If a foreign missionary having come to our land can feel so deeply for our people that he daily gives himself to pray for us with tears, then what he prays for must be very important. Let us join in prayer." Englund himself described prayer as a daily struggle, not with a God reluctant to bless but with a Devil reluctant to yield. He learned through experience that prayer overcomes stubborn human wills, breaks down prejudices, smashes demonic opposition and releases the power of God. Although the widespread revival of 1908-

1911 was not repeated on so great a scale, all through his long ministry William Englund saw the same sequence of events repeated time and time again in many churches. Conviction of sin was followed by confession and practical repentance, sometimes requiring restitution. Finally came the blessing of a closer fellowship with God, and between Christians, leading to an effective witness to those outside the Church.

Missionaries, struggling against incredible difficulties to establish a spiritual foothold in Shensi province in the 1890's, had seen their work brought to a standstill and almost wiped out by the terrible Boxer uprising in 1900 when they were all recalled to the Coast. The revival beginning in 1908 was also threatened by one of China's greatest upheavals.

Chinese resentment against their Manchu rulers had been rising faster and faster, and spilled over into a strong antiforeign movement. Two disastrous wars with Britain over the right to trade, primarily in opium, had been the beginning of an encroachment on China's sovereignty. The ancient Empire faced the agonizing choice between modernizing or becoming the spoil of nations she despised. Manchu rule was seen by men such as Dr. Sun Yat-sen to be the root cause of China's weakness and difficulties. If Heaven were slow to remove an unworthy occupant of the Dragon Throne, then revolutionaries must act. From 1907 to 1909 six uprisings were attempted in the South but all failed. In 1910, Canton, Hankow and even Peking staged abortive coups and, on October 10, 1911 the historic "Double Tenth," the Imperial garrison in Wuchang, mutinied. It was the spark which set all China aflame. The three-year-old emperor, Henry Pu Yi, abdicated. Imperial rule had ended; a republic was born.

On the same day as the nation was convulsed by revolution, God's people in Sian were overwhelmed by revival. Chinese Christians, seminary students, school children, missionaries and their families all experienced a fresh working of the Holy Spirit in their lives. Mr. E. R. Beckman who, with his wife, was in charge of the school for missionary children wrote, "more powerful meetings than these I have never before attended." But a sombre note was struck one evening when a young Chinese evangelist stood up and cried out, "There are many evil men in this city, and something terrible will happen. Pray, therefore, earnestly to the Lord."

The city was already in turmoil. The new governor was rumored to be away negotiating a mortgage on the oil wells for a foreign loan. At a hurriedly called public meeting it was determined to have the governor sliced in pieces on his return. At the same time, local troops threw in their lot with the revolutionaries and planned an attack on the Manchu quarter of the city.

Sunday, October 15 began ominously with an eclipse of the sun. It was like a curtain being drawn over 268 years of Manchu rule.

China was determined to control her own destiny. There was no room for the ruling Manchu, nor for any missionary or merchant from foreign lands. In Sian, resentment of missionaries burned in the heart of one man in particular. He was a police corporal. Mr. Beckman had rented a room for use as a chapel from a merchant in a suburb outside the south wall. A group of men, angry with the merchant for helping the missionary, broke into the chapel, dug through the wall into the adjoining store and stole his goods. Mr. Beckman reported the matter to the Manchu chief of police with the result that the corporal was charged with failing to protect the store, and ordered to refund the value of the stolen goods. Such a system obviously made for an efficient police force, but unknown to Beckman, the corporal was a member of the dreaded Ko-lao Hui, a secret society dedicated to the extermination of all foreigners, Manchu or missionary.

After conducting services in the west suburb that Sunday morning, Beckman returned to the school for missionary children. He was glad to find all was peaceful, but as he looked back over his shoulder he saw flames rising high from burning banks and Manchu homes. As darkness fell, the police corporal, thirsting for revenge, gathered a mob outside the city walls. Under pain of death he had ordered every family in his district to send a man to help destroy all mission property and kill all missionaries. At midnight the little school was surrounded. Flaming torches glinted on long knives, old swords, muskets and weapons of every kind. Men intoxicated with hatred yelled hoarsely for the death of all "foreign devils." Inside the walls of the school compound, faith and fear fought a desperate battle in the hearts of missionaries and children. Prayer, sobbed out to God, was almost drowned by bloodthirsty screams of the mob. Desperate plans for escape were made. Under cover of darkness, Chinese helpers had already found a way out over the back wall. But, in the hurried confusion, Beckman could not find the ladder they had used and frantically tried to dig through the wall. Suddenly, with a yell of triumph, the rioters burst in. Mrs. Beckman tenderly bent to kiss her youngest child. Then she and her husband were abruptly separated, engulfed in a torrent of undeserved malice. And only when Mr. Wilhelm Vatne, the young school teacher, Mrs. Beckman, and six missionary children lay dead, was the fury of the mob abated. Mr. Beckman, and his youngest daughter, Thyra, miraculously escaped. One of the young martyrs was George, the ten-year-old son of Mr. and Mrs. G. Ahlstrand. God had spoken to him during the Sian revival, and he had tearfully confessed to beating his dog. When his brokenhearted parents found his mutilated body lying in the open fields, the dog was faithfully standing guard beside him.

William and Lena Englund were spared the horrors of those bloody days of revolution. Furlough had taken them back to the United States, but now they were ready to return.

4

"Whoever receives one child in my name receives me"

As William and Lena Englund once more sailed westward across the blue Pacific they faced a China in travail. A republic was struggling to come to birth. Sun Yat-sen had resigned as its first president, to be replaced by Yuan Shih-kai who had secret hopes of one day ascending in the Dragon Throne and establishing himself as founder of a new Chinese imperial dynasty. Scraps of news from Shensi province were not encouraging. Revolution had not brought peace to the Northwest. Armies with shifting loyalties ravaged the countryside; robber bands roamed at will. For Englund and his wife, returning to China was harder than the first time when the hardships of pioneer evangelism, difficulties of the work, and dangers from sickness and political disorders were either unknown or overlooked in the exhilaration of being called to carry the gospel to the people of another nation. Now they knew that ahead of them was the hard reality of drought, famine, death-dealing typhus, poisonous scorpions, bedbugs, uncomfortable travel over roads that were either mud or dust, and a thousand other hardships, which could all have been easily avoided simply by remaining in America. Above all, there was the capricious mood of the masses, as unpredictable as the wind. Sun Yat-sen had been educated in a mission school in Hawaii where he had made a Christian profession, but whether the new provincial government in Shensi would be favorable to missionaries or not, no one knew. All that was certain was God's wisdom, power and presence to aid them.

Home again in Lantien, the Englunds rejoiced to find that the revolution had not stopped revival. A very pleasant part of their responsibility was the care of two primary schools for girls and boys. Evangelical missionaries have sometimes been ignorantly criticized for doing nothing but preach the gospel to people who need food, clothes and shelter. Facts prove the opposite. From the beginning, missionaries showed a practical concern for the physical needs of people. Like Jesus Himself, they were moved with compassion at the sight of the multitudes. Schools, medical clinics, hospitals, orphanages and famine relief demonstrated their concern.

Lena and William Englund both had a love for children. Lena could never forget her first visit to Chenchiakou village. At the terrifying sight of her (a foreign woman), everyone had fled except a very old lady and a little girl, whom nobody wanted because of an ugly growth on her forehead. Peering through windows and cracks in the doors, people had watched to see the fate of the two victims. Smiling, Lena walked towards the child. As the distance between them diminished, so did the girl's tears. It was not only Lena's Chinese clothes and fluency in the language that bridged the gap. For the first time in her life the child was being loved and in her heart she instinctively knew it. Lena invited her to the house where she was staying, and with their wildest fears confirmed, the villagers saw the two disappear behind the strong wooden door. "Now she will dig out her heart to make foreign medicine," they whispered to each other, warning their own children to keep silent lest they too be discovered.

"God also loves you," Lena explained gently. "He proved that by sending His only Son to this earth to die for us. But after three days in the grave, He rose from the dead, and now lives in Heaven where He listens to our prayers. He forgives those who believe in Him, and makes them His forever." The little girl listened, faith opening up in her heart like a rosebud in summer. "But the lump on my head?" she asked. "Doctors have cut it out many times but it always grows again. Can Jesus take it away?" "I'm sure He can," Lena answered, and prayed with the child. Then, as the whimsical idea struck her, she fastened an obviously foreign adhesive strip over the growth so that everyone would know that the girl had actually been touched by a missionary, and sent her home. The girl ran gaily out of the door to be surrounded almost immediately by a curious crowd. "What did she do to you? Has your heart been dug out? Does she have devil's eyes so that she can see right through you?" they asked. The child laughed. "I still have my heart," she replied, "and somebody lives in there now—Jesus, God's Son." As the girl answered their questions, one woman, more inquisitive than the rest, had been pulling at the adhesive strip. When it came loose, the crowd gasped. The ugly lump was completely gone and it never grew again. Later, Lena Englund saw that girl become a fine, well-trained Bible woman.

William Englund, too, enjoyed children as much as they enjoyed him. His bubbling humor, his enthusiasm, his imagination and, above all, his tender love for God's little people won him countless friends. Few could equal him as a storyteller. He had begun at an early age.

In school races his short legs always brought him in last, but in imaginative tales, no one could keep up with him. There had been a day when the howling of distant wolves had terrified him on his way home through the forest near St. Hilaire, Minnesota, but as he dashed into the log cabin, all out of breath, he had a dramatic story on his tongue. His mother's blue eyes had opened wide in horror as her little son described the gigantic wolf, leading a ferocious pack of long fanged, snarling beasts across the path only a few paces from the resolute hero.

Englund did not yet have children of his own to delight with colorfully told Bible stories, and he had still to meet the intensely personal problem of balancing responsibilities of a father with those of a missionary evangelist and Bible teacher. But he already had a tender understanding of children, to which they eagerly responded. Many years later, a grandson summed up his generation's evaluation of William Englund by announcing, "Grandpa's a cool guy!"

The little Chinese boys and girls attending primary school in Lantien might have put the same sentiment into a somewhat more classical form. Most of them were orphans, or came from very poor homes where they could not be cared for properly. The most important part of the education Englund gave them was instruction in the Scriptures. And when revival swept through parts of Shensi, God did not overlook the needs of children. Sitting in his study, Englund was startled to hear the evening quiet broken by the sound of loud sobbing, which seemed to come from the direction of the boy's dormitory. When he hurried to see what was the matter an astonishing sight met his eyes. No one had spoken to the boys, but God's Spirit had smitten them down, like a tornado bowling over a forest of saplings. Childish sins, enormous to their awakened consciences, were being confessed as they knelt together and with flowing tears, they pleaded for forgiveness. William Englund gently directed them all to Jesus Christ and His cross where an eternal remedy could be found. No sooner had the little fellows found relief in the Savior's death than Englund again heard the sound of loud crying, this time from the girl's dormitory. Running over there, he found a similar scene.

The events of that evening were not merely an emotional outburst by immature children. Many of them, in the mundane atmosphere of the classroom, later confessed to their teachers that they had lied and cheated, and poor though they were, they determined to give for the work of the Lord. Their problem was easily reduced to a single question. How does one give when he has no money? The matter was discussed at great length and with much earnestness. "Listen," said one little boy. "For breakfast we have rice soup and bread. If we gave up the bread, the money saved could be our gift to God." Never did a group of boys with normal hearty appetites agree more willingly to go without food. And the teacher was informed of their unanimous decision. A few days later, Englund watched one of the smallest boys standing in the school yard enjoying his morning bowl of soup. The missionary's breakfast of fruit juice, choice of cereal, bacon, eggs, hotcakes and syrup, with a glass or two of milk would have been a fantasy beyond the boy's wildest imaginings. Englund walked across the yard and bent down to ask him, "Don't you regret making that pledge? Now you have only soup and no bread." The little fellow turned his black sparkling eyes up to his questioner. "No, I don't regret it one little bit," he answered. "Jesus Christ suffered much more for me."

Revival among the school children did more than eliminate cheating and lying from the classroom, and stimulate sacrificial giving. God's Spirit laid the spiritual foundation for a life of Christian service. By 1914 Englund was able to report that the schools for boys and girls had produced three evangelists, three Bible women, one school teacher and added 28 believers to the Lantien church. And even during their school years God used the children in wonderful ways. One evening as Englund was having vespers with the boys and girls, a blind man walked in, attracted by the singing. He had never been in a church or heard of Christ, but listened attentively to God's offer of life, joy and hope through faith in the Savior. The blind man hesitated a moment and then poured out his story. Well educated, he had been a teacher until his sight failed. For a time he lived on his savings, but when these were exhausted, he visited his brothers to ask their help. They turned him away and, in despair, he had decided to return home and somehow raise enough money to buy poison and kill himself. The shocked children whose songs had diverted the blind man from his terrible purpose knelt with Englund to pray for him. To their amazement the blind man also broke out in prayer. With no one to instruct him, and without any knowledge of Christian terms, he stumbled through as best he could, often using Buddhist phrases. But he knew what he wanted, and God who reads the thoughts and intents of the heart understood and came into his life.

The blind man's first concern was his family, especially a daughter for whom he had arranged a marriage with a neighboring family. The betrothal had been arranged when the girl was very young because her family urgently needed the dowry which Chinese custom required the bridegroom's family to pay. Marriage had not yet taken place but the little girl was already living in her future mother-in-law's home where she was treated no better than a slave. In spite of having feet bound so tightly that she could hardly walk, she was daily sent out into the fields to do a man's work. "This poor girl also needs our prayers," said Englund, as once more he knelt with the children and the blind man.

Long and complicated negotiations with the bridegroom's family began. It was finally agreed that the girl would be returned to her father if the dowry were paid back in full. Glad to be part of the answer to his own prayers and moved by his tender heart, Englund himself paid. The grateful father, led by a boy, went to get his daughter only to be met with a thousand objections and fresh arguments. All day the battle of words waged. As evening came, the obdurate family tried to persuade the blind father to spend the night in their home. But prayer was answered. The family suddenly yielded and father and daughter walked out of the house. Realizing that the girl could not possibly reach Lantien on her tiny feet, the father hoisted her on his back and guided through the darkness by the faithful boy began the long journey.

Vespers had ended, boys and girls were hurrying around and doing the seemingly endless things children find necessary before going to bed, when suddenly they were startled by a shout at the door. There was the blind man, soaked with perspiration. Englund looked at him without realizing the reason for his condition. "What's the matter," he asked. "Did you fall into a stream?." "No," he answered, laughing and crying, "she was so heavy." The daughter was put into school, and afterwards married a fine Christian man. The father was Englund's language teacher for a time, and with his intimate knowledge of the Chinese classics was able to give him a deeper insight into Chinese philosophy. But the blind man's taste had changed. He memorized many long Scripture passages and became an effective evangelist. He never tired of telling how the songs of children had attracted him to Christ on the very night he had decided to end his life.

In their concern for children, William and Lena had not forgotten their responsibilities to the Lantien church. The results of revival continued there too. Between 1906 and 1915, membership increased from 15 to 241. Englund had followed a basic mission policy of training Chinese Christians so that responsibility for the work could be passed on to them. Pioneer evangelism was no longer solely in the hands of missionaries, but in Lantien was shared with ten evangelists, four Bible women, two colporteurs and four unpaid helpers. Within the church, the Englunds worked together with their Chinese brothers and sisters as an effective team.

Now a long dark shadow came reaching out towards William Englund. Late in the year 1916 he and Lena decided to go to Shanghai for a medical checkup. A generation born in hospitals, growing up with full health insurance, accustomed to the sound of ambulances speeding to emergencies, and faced with the dilemma of choosing a physician from the hundreds listed in a telephone directory, must surely have difficulty in appreciating the health problems of missionary pioneers seventy years ago. Physical hazards were so great that some mission boards did not expect more than one term of service from their China missionaries, if hopefully they survived that. In many areas there were local Chinese doctors who had trained themselves by carefully studying the ancient books of medicine. Their tribal remedies could be surprisingly effective, but the herbalist himself was rather more successful in selling his mysterious products than in making a diagnosis. Among the many carefully wrapped packets in a village store was one noticeably larger than the rest. When the proprietor was asked the reason for this, he stroked his wisp of a beard and slowly replied, "Now and then someone comes along with a variety of rather unclear symptoms, and I'm not ten-tenths sure what the exact cause is. That large package contains a little of almost every herb I have. When in doubt, I give the customer that!"

For serious illness and major surgery no help was available. With sensitive fingers, the local barber using wire ear cleaners could remove wax. Acupuncture practitioners followed the ancient art of injecting long needles in appropriate parts of the body, and claimed to be able to effect marvelous cures, but a missionary was often faced with a difficult choice. He could trust God to heal miraculously, with or without any remedies on hand. He could take the risk of adding the perils and difficulties of travel to the dangers of a serious sickness, and journey to the provincial capital or some other place where foreign hospitals had been established. Or he could send for aid, knowing that by the time the message reached the doctor and the help arrived, the patient would either be recovered or dead.

Lena Englund had not been feeling well for several months. She and her husband stayed at the spacious headquarters of the China Inland Mission in the Shanghai International Settlement. The doctors were not satisfied with their first examinations and advised her to remain for further tests. She and William agreed that it would be best for him to return to Lantien where so much needed to be done. With his thoughts and prayers continually for his wife, he once more plunged into the work. Not long before Christmas, it was necessary for him to visit the provincial capital of Sian on mission business. As he bumped along the dusty road in an old wooden cart, he began praying earnestly for his wife. He seemed to hear a voice telling him that a telegram was awaiting him, and shortly afterwards a messenger from the Mission Center arrived with a telegram. Lena's condition had worsened and the doctors advised his immediate return to Shanghai. He left without a moment's delay.

Englund found his wife critically ill with a kidney infection and edema. As instinctively as a bird seeks shelter from an approaching storm, he turned to God. Kneeling beside her bed, he prayed that she might be delivered from her terrible suffering. Her heart grew weaker and breathing more difficult. Only as William supported her in his strong arms was she able to draw in desperate gasps of air, and so the long hours of darkness passed, husband and wife bound together in tender love and deepest suffering. With dawn came a severe heart attack. Lena turned her face towards her beloved William and whispered her loving farewell, and still in his arms, fell asleep in Jesus. Years later, Englund, who was not a man to exaggerate, testified that Lena had led 10,000 persons to Christ during her remarkable ministry.

5

"He endured as seeing Him who is invisible"

His sorrow and loneliness being acute, far from his native land, Englund resolutely returned to Shensi. With sympathetic understanding, Mr. Bengtsson, principal of the theological seminary, opened his home to his old friend. But his heart was in Lantien, a place of happy memories now made poignant by the loss of his wife, and there he began to visit frequently. Almost immediately he was again in the shadow of death.

Revolution and banditry continued to spread misery and terror. For most people the only certainties of life were fear and bloodshed. Soldiers at the city gate did not bar his entry, but as he entered the church courtyard one of the elders hurried to tell him in shocked whispers that a terrible thing had happened. "Pastor I, the soldiers now holding the city are rebels," he said. "They seized power two days ago. During the shooting many people crowded into the church for safety. Our beloved brother Yang took this as an opportunity of preaching the gospel to them. As he stood in the pulpit earnestly exhorting everyone to trust in Christ, a soldier stomped in, marched to the front, looked at brother Yang and said, "You are the preacher here, are you?" And then shot him through the heart." The elder paused a moment, and then asked, "You will preach to us this morning, Pastor I? The people have already gathered for worship." Many thoughts flashed through Englund's mind: solemn thoughts of the cost of following Jesus Christ; comforting thoughts that the dead in Christ would be raised at His coming; encouraging thoughts that a martyr's blood is never spilt in vain. "I am ready to share God's Word with you," he answered and entered the church with the elder. When called on to speak, Englund walked to the pulpit and found himself standing on the dark bloodstains of a much loved brother in Christ.

Near Lantien was a range of mountains known as a stronghold for robbers. The only protection against them was soldiers, of which there were several categories. They might be government troops, conscripts of a provincial army, retainers of a local warlord or mercenaries preparing for the more lucrative profession of a bandit.

The gospel had been bravely taken into this wild country and a small chapel built. Englund was there hoping for two weeks of quiet retreat with Chinese church leaders and workers. He stepped out of the inn where he was staying, thankful to be alive after a noisy night in which the mountain town had been invaded by a powerful force of bandits, and strategically abandoned by soldiers. Englund did not know exactly what had taken place and made his way to the early morning prayer meeting. That ended, he began walking back to the inn. He was wearing a khaki-colored summer suit. Down the street, a bandit on the lookout for soldier stragglers grabbed his gun and took careful aim. As his finger pressed slowly on the trigger one of his comrades yelled, "What are you doing? Shooting a foreign missionary?" The bandit lowered his rifle, and the following day came to apologize to Englund for his mistake, and to promise him protection as long as he was in the mountains.

In his second letter to the Corinthians, Paul is remarkably frank in telling of his thoughts and feelings. He had been preserved from 'imminent death," was "knocked down but never knocked out," and had been "completely overwhelmed." Significantly, he speaks in the same letter of his travels in which he had been in constant danger from rivers, floods, bandits, from his own countrymen and from pagans. Paul also reveals the secret of his power of endurance by saying that "this is the ministry which God in his mercy has given us and nothing can daunt us." William Englund was traveling the same road. No journey was without difficulty or danger of some sort. But neither man nor demon could rob him of the treasure of God's Word which he was determined to share with all who would listen. His high calling outweighed the appalling difficulties and discouragements of those turbulent days of China's history.

Even non-Christians recognized in Englund the courage and fortitude which God had welded into his character. As he returned on horseback to Lantien one day he was surprised to be met by a delegation of city elders. "Our city was attacked by a powerful band of robbers and our mandarin suddenly remembered that he had most urgent business in another place. He left hurriedly and has not returned. Now we have no one to take care of our city affairs," they explained. "You have been here a long time, and we all know you and have confidence in you. Would you kindly take over the mandarin's position, and be our leader?" Times had surely changed from earlier days when missionaries had been met with a barrage of stones, taunts and threats. But Englund had no ambitions for civic office. He courteously thanked the elders for their invitation, and explained that he had come to China to preach Christ, and not to rule over cities. He also gave practical help by dismounting from his horse and praying right there in the main street that God would bring the mandarin back and restore the city to normal. And in the mysterious working of God, even in the hearts of those who do not know Him, the mandarin returned promptly.

Shensi provided other difficulties to test a man's endurance; some of them tinged with subtle humor that appealed to Englund even when he suffered from it. Travel in those days was usually by horse, mule litter, or Chinese cart. The bicycle was still a novelty rarely seen. Whatever views Englund may have had on the subject of transportation, the Chinese greatly preferred that he ride his marvelous "foot-pedaling-cart," which balanced so miraculously when in motion and fell so helplessly when stopped. But the advantage of its incredible speed was sometimes lost if Englund had to stop to ask directions. A crowd would immediately gather to inspect the amazing foreign contraption. After their curiosity had been somewhat satisfied, the friendly audience would engage in a long and animated discussion, punctuated with many smiles, as to the best route for the rider to take. When Englund mounted his bicycle to resume the journey with long and complicated directions to follow, he was often bewildered to find that he had made an enormous detour through numerous villages before reaching his destination. Eventually he caught on to what was happening. Those who gave him directions wanted all their friends and relatives to see the incredible sight of a foreign gentleman riding his two wheeled contraption, and therefore routed him by the most roundabout way possible.

Englund perhaps wished that he was riding his bicycle; he could have escaped the two men coming resolutely towards him with obviously evil intentions. Piercing winter winds and snow had forced him to hire a cart, springless but new. An invitation had come for a Bible conference in a church some distance from Sian. He knew that travel would be dangerous because the town had recently fallen into the hands of a rebel leader whose soldiers were graduates from a career of banditry. He was made even more vulnerable to attack by being asked to carry a large sum of money urgently needed by fellow missionaries working in the area. The rebel soldiers reined in beside the lumbering cart. "Do you have any money?" they demanded. Englund's eyes opened wide in surprise. "Who do you suppose would carry money in days so unsafe as these," he parried. The men insisted on searching the baggage. They opened the suitcase, carefully examined all the books, took out the clothes and kept them and pounced on an old watch which had belonged to Englund's father. In answer to prayer made before the journey began, the soldiers ignored a small bag containing all the money, evidently thinking it contained nothing of value. Then they rode away, leaving Englund to follow slowly in his cart. The money was safe, clothes could somehow be replaced, but the loss of his father's watch was hard to bear.

Glad to see their beloved Pastor I again, the Christians listened as he told of his unpleasant adventure along the way, and decided to change the evening program. "First, we must pray that the Lord will get all Pastor I's clothes back, and that watch which belonged to his old father. Then we will have the time of Bible teaching," they said. The following day, an officer from the rebel forces called on Englund, whom he had previously met. When he heard the story of the robbery, he suggested that a visit to army headquarters would have good results. With that encouragement, Englund and a fellow missionary did so and were courteously received. "We can be pretty sure who troubled you," the officers told them. "We will make an investigation." Two days later everything was restored including the precious watch.

The word "exciting" is not to be found in Englund's letters to his many friends. He was not looking for adventure in China, but seeking for men to bring to Christ. The sorrows, dangers and difficulties he endured were to that end. Like a strong swimmer forging ahead through stormy seas and treacherous currents to rescue a drowning man, Englund persisted in the spiritual rescue operation to which God had called him, and whenever anyone was delivered from darkness and death, his joy was unbounded.

The dark old-fashioned clothes, and long hair poked through a hole in his black cap, identified the man as a Taoist priest. He listened intently as Englund described Christ's sufferings and death on the Cross for the sins of all mankind. He returned the second evening to hear more. And on the third night, as Englund stood up to preach, the priest left his seat at the back of the church and walked forward. "Please, I would like to ask a question," he said. "Do you think that Jesus Christ would want a person such as I?" Englund smiled. "Yes, of course. Christ came especially to save sinners, and you are one. He came to save you," he answered. But the priest was not convinced. For many years he had made pilgrimages from temple to temple seeking an elusive peace. As soon as he heard the gospel he realized that he had made the tragic mistake of seeking in the wrong place, like a man spending a lifetime in a coal mine digging for jade and becoming blind in his futile search. He doubted that Jesus Christ would have a welcome for one who had been so foolish. From his pocket he produced two long nails. "Two evenings ago you told us that Christ Jesus was nailed to a cross for us," he said. "If He will accept me, then I am willing for my hands to be nailed." Deeply moved, Englund looked at the old priest. If a man could be so hungry for God that he was willing to suffer the pain of crucified hands, then was it not worth every discomfort and danger to bring the gospel to him?

Englund explained that the nails were unnecessary since self imposed suffering cannot make a man more acceptable to God. "The sacrifice of Jesus Christ on the Cross was perfect and complete. He left nothing unfinished. All you need to do is to accept Him thankfully as your Savior," he said. But the priest was determined that his own hands should be nailed. "At least nail one of my hands," he suggested. Englund asked for the nails, and the old priest gave them up thinking that his pitiful request was about to be granted. But Englund put them in his pocket, and praying that the Lord would open the eyes of the old man, gently requested him to return to his seat. Through all the service, the Taoist priest sat silent, tears rolling down his face. Then a Chinese evangelist, particularly gifted and warm of heart, sat beside the old man to explain more fully the meaning of Christ's death.

The following evening the priest was again in church, his face radiant. "How do you feel today? Do you have peace at last?" Englund asked. "Yes, indeed, I have peace in my heart," he replied. When asked how it had happened, he answered, "Now I understand that Christ died on the Cross as my substitute. I have accepted Him, and He has given me peace." Englund took the nails out of his pocket, and asked, "What about these? Do you need them today?" The old man smiled. "I have no need of nails now. Now I understand that long ago nails in the hands of Jesus Christ when He hung on the Cross were for me."

At such times many a missionary has asked himself what would have happened if he had succumbed to the temptation to take life easy and not come to another land. Englund certainly was willing to endure the hardships of a missionary career for the joy of seeing men and women, boys and girls find forgiveness and new life in Christ.

6

A Wider Ministry

The Sian school for missionary children was rebuilt in 1915, four years after its total destruction in the year of the Revolution. Ingeborg Hanaberg, a nurse and member of the Salem Evangelical Free Church in Chicago, arrived in China in 1913 and after a period of language study was appointed a teacher in the school. In May 1919, the Lord gave her to William Englund as a helpmate. After their marriage, they made their home in Lantien for the year before furlough. Ingeborg's parents were Norwegian, and after a short visit in America with friends in Chicago, the Englunds sailed the Atlantic so that she could be in her old home in Norway for the birth of their first child.

Englund immediately followed his lifelong passion for preaching the Scriptures. Even after speaking almost nothing but Chinese for more than 15 years, he had no difficulty in switching to Norwegian. The pattern of revival which he had seen in China was repeated in Norway. In the city of Kristiansand, for example, during special services held for two weeks in the cathedral and a church hall, 200 people were converted.

In May, 1921 William and Ingeborg Englund returned to America with their baby daughter Miriam. Rev. C. T. Dyrness, pastor of Salem Evangelical Free Church, had been invited to spend a year in Norway, and Englund accepted a call to fill his place in Chicago. The congregation was largely Scandinavian in background. Services were held both in Norwegian and English.

But for Englund, China, not Chicago, was home. Shensi tugged at his heart continually and in the fall of 1922 he and his wife once more crossed the Pacific and settled down in Lantien. For one-year-old Miriam everything was a brand new experience.

Revolutionaries were discovering that it was much more difficult to establish a new order than to destroy the old. Sun Yat-sen, still struggling to bring the republic to birth, could not return even to his own headquarters in Canton until his forces won a victory there in December, 1922. The same month Adolf Joffe, representing the Soviet Union, visited Shanghai for discussions with Dr. Sun. Clearly Russia's part was playing the role of champion of the Chinese cause, professing sympathy for their aim to make the country strong and independent. On his part, Dr. Sun wanted to discover if Soviet ideas could be adapted to the needs of his People's Party, the Kuomintang.

As a result of the talks, Sun Yat-sen sent his Chief of Staff, Chiang Kai-shek, on a four month visit to the U.S.S.R., where he visited naval and military establishments, and a chemical warfare center. The Soviet Union gained further favor by being the first nation to recognize China as an equal. Their ambassador, Leo Karakhan, arrived in Peking in 1924. Michael Borodin appeared on the scene the same year. Born in Russia, he had been taken to the U.S. as a child and educated there. Shortening his original name from Gruzenberg to Berg, he opened a business school in Chicago. Later, inspired by the 1917 Russian revolution, he changed it again and became Borodin. After preaching revolution in Mexico, experiencing dismal failure in Scotland and most unsuccessful efforts in Turkey, he arrived in Canton with a letter of recommendation from Ambassador Karakhan. His charming personality won him the position of advisor to the Kuomintang. His persuasiveness won the Chinese Communist Party a place in the Kuomintang.

Chiang Kai-shek was one of the first to feel the impact of these political moves. Sun Yat-sen was desperately aware of the need of well-trained and trustworthy military leaders, and in 1924 opened the Whampoa Military Academy with Chiang Kai-shek as its first president. Chou En-lai, a founding member of the Communist Party, was head of the Academy's political department. General Bluecher (also known as Galens) headed a staff of Russian instructors. From the beginning friction was strong between members of the Kuomintang, the communist staff and the cadets. At the same time the new philosophy was being preached in Hunan province with fanatical enthusiasm. The strong voice of Mao Tse-tung, throbbing with bitter hatred, was calling men to follow him to a better way of life. His immediate goal was to head the provincial Communist Party. He had already organized 22 trade unions, including key movements against coal miners, printers, railroadmen and students. He was now 30 years old. The spiritual battle for China had taken a new turn.

The restless Northwest felt repercussions from the violent political struggles in South and Central China. The antiforeign spirit of the terrible Boxers had not died out with the passing of Manchu rule. Calling themselves "Hard Bellies" (Ying Tu-tzu), "Red Spears" or simply, "Old Brothers" (Ko-lao Hui), they spread terror through Shensi province. After more than a quarter of a century of incessant war, banditry, bloodshed and suffering, weary missionaries asked each other if peace would ever come. They daily faced the stark reality of "not contending against flesh and blood, but against the principalities, against the powers, against the world rulers of this present darkness, against the spiritual hosts of wickedness in the heavenly places." The Devil, whose only occupation is destruction, had launched a full-scale attack not only on missionaries and the Chinese church, but on all who might be brought from death to life through faith in Christ.

The Englunds had hardly arrived back in Lantien when the local magistrate sent his family to the mission station for safety. The "Hard Bellies" were preparing to attack the city, and although the magistrate had posted soldiers around the walls, he evidently had more faith in the God of the foreigners than in the guns of his men. One of his little sons evidently held the same view, for as soon as he entered the mission compound he said to his mother, "Now we can feel safe because we have come where Jesus is."

Encouraged by the kindness shown his family, the magistrate came with another request to Englund. He did not want to inconvenience Pastor I, but he would certainly be most thankful if he would take the trouble to go out and persuade the Hard Bellies to go away. "I am sorry," replied Englund, "but talking with demon possessed men is useless. Speaking with God is the only way of deliverance, and this I will do." The Hard Bellies, believing they had a magical immunity to bullets, attacked the east gate of the city. Inside the mission compound Christians prayed. On the walls, the defending soldiers fired with remarkable accuracy, and the Hard Bellies who survived the slaughter fled in disorder. Soon after this fresh experience of God's protective care, Englund and his wife were asked to move to the capital city of Sian.

More than 30 years of pioneer evangelism, systematic Bible teaching and courageous faith had resulted in a church of over 500 members. Peter Holmen had been the first to sing and pray his way into Sian city in 1892. His precarious foothold was threatened when a mob gathered to drive him out of a rented house. Before the crowd had time to attack, Holmen opened the door and courteously invited them in to drink tea. Outmaneuvered by being treated as guests, they listened quietly while Holmen played his guitar and sang every gospel song he knew in Chinese, Norwegian and English.

But the one man concert was nothing compared to the arrival of four missionary women a year and a half later. Chinese women by the wagonload poured into the city from all directions to see the remarkable sight of ladies whose hair was yellow, eyes blue and feet enormous. That they all wore Chinese gowns in no way diminished the novelty of their appearance. Two years after his arrival in Sian, Hol-

42

men died of typhoid as he was on his way to meet his fiancée from Norway.

After a long absence, E. R. Beckman returned to China. The Chinese government had given him a considerable sum of money as an expression of their sympathy in the loss of his wife and two children when the missionary school had been attacked. He used the gift to buy the residence of a wealthy Chinese family in the northern part of Sian and converted it into a chapel and mission home. When William and Ingeborg Englund moved into the city, the suburban church had nearly 250 members.

Englund's new responsibilities were considerable. He was treasurer for his own mission, and for 100 missionaries of other societies working in the Northwest. This not only involved receiving and transmitting funds, and keeping accurate accounts, but also a steady flow of correspondence with the Mission headquarters in Chicago. He was language examiner for new missionaries. He was also expected to give some attention to a bookstore and printing press, but none of these duties kept him from his life goal of preaching and teaching. He found comfort in the old Danish proverb, "It is difficult to trap the eel and hunt the hare at the same time," and wrote home, "To go fishing is our first priority, however, there is no doubt that letter writing is the hare than runs away while we are working with the slippery eel." He was, in fact, ministering to 20 churches and preaching centers with a total membership of about 1,000, but he accepted his other responsibilities as an assignment from God and not as an unwelcome imposition. In a Swedish letter to friends, Englund wrote that his ministry had doubled. As far as spiritual and business matters were concerned, this was somewhat an understatement. As far as his responsibilities as a father were concerned, it was strictly accurate, for soon after William and Ingeborg settled in Sian, God gave them a second daughter, Grace.

Englund's gifts as a Bible teacher and preacher had become recognized. In Sian he was free from the pastoral responsibility of any one particular church, and increasing calls came to him as a conference speaker. He somehow found time to accept invitations to Hsingping and Lantien, as well as to speak at a conference of the Sian churches. In every case, the schedule was heavy. In Hsingping, for example, Englund preached 16 times in eight days. The Lord had wonderfully used Rev. and Mrs. Solomon Bergstrom in the development of the church there. From 1913 to 1923 membership had grown to nearly 1,500; 11 other smaller churches and 13 preaching centers had been established in the district. All the churches were represented at the conference, which was attended by about 800 people, meeting for two sessions daily.

Visits to Lantien were always a highlight for Englund, and the church always responded warmly to the ministry of their beloved

43

Pastor I En-cheng.

A poor wheat harvest had sent prices soaring. To make ends meet, farmers were openly growing opium poppies along the roadside, unafraid of loud official threats of the death penalty and encouraged by secret bribes from the same source of six Chinese dollars an acre. Englund had heard that a Christian widow, living near Lantien, had been publicly beaten and fined for refusing to support the local Buddhist temple and take part in a festival of idol worship, and her son had been thrown into prison. Traveling the familiar road towards the city, he wondered if drought, high prices and official hostility would keep people from the conference and tent evangelism in the area.

He need not have been anxious. People came from all directions, including a little old lady who stomped along on bound feet for 30 miles. Four times a day the church was packed and four times a day revival fell like spring rains on parched ground. In the villages, people crowded into the large tent to hear the gospel. At least 50 men and women turned from idols to serve the living and true God. Among them was a young man, strongly antagonistic to Christ, for whom many had prayed. When he fell down the stairs in his home, injuring his foot so badly that he had to lie in bed for a month, no one saw the accident as a means God could use to answer prayer for his salvation. But hopping down the church aisle to be baptized, the young man testified that the injury was the best thing that had ever happened to him. While he had been confined to the quietness of his bedroom, God had broken down all opposition and brought him to Himself.

Englund took advantage of the journey back to Sian to catch up on some of his correspondence. "It's rather enjoyable in the loneliness here on the cart to come in contact with dear friends on the other side of the earth," he wrote. "Of course, we do get in contact with you through the Heavenly Central Switchboard, but to be able to write is a great joy. Most of the way has been terribly full of dust, so that I haven't dared to take out the typewriter. We ourselves have almost gotten buried in dust." The letter closed with the hope that their daughter Grace would one day be a missionary, but, wrote Englund, "this will take time as she is still only four months old."

Back in the Capital, he was glad to find the churches humming with activity. Chinese evangelists and Bible women were moving out in all directions with the message of new life in Christ. A student from the seminary had obtained permission for ten days of tent meetings in his home town, where he was the only Christian and bitterly opposed by his father. Some of his fellow students, playing vigorously on their brass instruments, helped to draw a crowd, but victory was really won down by the riverside where morning by morning the young preacher wrestled in prayer. One evening his heart nearly burst with joy as he saw his parents accept Christ, and then offer their home as a meeting place for the new believers, 26 in all. His father later gave a piece of land for building a church.

William Englund was experiencing a personal problem. He was beginning to have trouble with his hearing. Other members of his family had known similar difficulties and the matter was all the more serious because he needed a finely tuned sense of hearing to distinguish between subtle differences in Chinese words.

As the spring of 1924 approached, Englund met with another physical setback. Two weeks of a serious sinus infection weakened him greatly, forcing him to decline an invitation to speak at the Sian church conference. But by the end of April, happy and excited, he was able to accompany his wife to the English Baptist Hospital in Sian for the birth of their third child. "This time perhaps a son," he said with a smile as they parted. Englund, according to his custom when deep in thought or prayer, paced up and down as he waited for good news of the child's birth. In the delivery room doctors and nurses struggled with unexpected complications and difficulties. Ingeborg's heart began to show signs of strain. The doctor quickly turned his attention to her, but in a shattering crisis both mother and unborn child died.

For Ingeborg, God's call had not been unexpected. A few days earlier she had a premonition that she would soon be in the presence of the Lord. But for William Englund, the loss of a beloved wife, and shattered hopes of a son to follow in his footsteps, was like a sword thrust in his tender heart. The old familiar streets of Sian were blurred by tears as he made his way back to the Mission Center where two little girls were waiting excitedly to know if they had a baby brother or sister. Without himself understanding the mysterious ways of God, Englund gently drew the children to him and quietly explained that their mother was at home with Jesus, and had taken the baby with her. For two-year-old Grace the words had little meaning. Their impact would come slowly as day followed day without a mother to pray over her, tuck her into bed and kiss her goodnight, but as Miriam listened to the shattering news, she looked up into her father's face and said, "I want to go to Jesus, too." And William Englund, borne down by grief and the responsibility of caring for his two little daughters, knew not what to do except look up into his Father's face. "We look for the breaking of the day when every shadow shall flee away, and everything shall be clear in the light of His glory," he wrote.

Officially, The Evangelical Alliance Mission is an organization whose object is "religious, philanthropic and educational, designed to form a missionary agency representing churches, societies and individuals for spreading the Gospel of our Lord Jesus Christ and establishing, developing and promoting all phases of church work in foreign lands." Its members discover that it is more than that. From experience they know it to be a family, tightly bound together by love and mutual concern, and when Englund arrived at the annual Field Conference with his two little daughters, his fellow missionaries were waiting with sympathy and practical help. The women took care of Miriam and Grace. Herman Swenson invited Englund and his two girls to travel back to Sian with him and his family, never imagining that he himself would see two of his children die of dysentery along the way. And in Sian, Ruth Anderson, a nurse, volunteered to take care of Englund's daughters, but within a year she was struck down with sickness and taken to be with Christ. Mr. and Mrs. Nils Jacobsen then offered to share their home with Englund and his daughters. With family problems settled, he once more resolutely turned to the task for which God had called him to China. His ministry entered a new phase when he accepted a call to replace Rev. and Mrs. Olav Bengtsson, who were returning to Sweden after being in charge of the Sian Seminary for 20 years.

7

Urgent out of Season

If William Englund had been a man who could minister only when conditions were favorable and times quiet, he would have had few opportunities in China. In fact, revival fire burned so constantly in his heart that he seldom needed exhortation to "preach the Word; be urgent in season, out of season."

Conditions in 1925 could not have been much worse. Dr. Sun Yat-sen died without seeing his vision of a united, independent and prosperous China fulfilled. For more than five years as many as 30 areas of the country had been under the absolute control of warlords. Violence reigned, striking impartially. Mao Tse-tung was fleeing from his native Hunan with a price on his head. The province had been seized by a mercenary general, impatient with agitators and quick to cut short their careers with a bullet through the neck. On May 25 of that year, a British officer in Shanghai ordered police in the International Settlement to fire on students and workers protesting the arrest of some laborers. Twelve students were killed and strikes and antiforeign demonstrations broke out all over China. Strong propaganda was directed at Christian schools and restrictive laws passed which threatened to close their doors.

Sian, an Imperial city second only to Peking, did not escape the national turmoil. General Sung Cheh-yuan, whose allegiance was to Wu Pei-fu, later to hold office under Mao Tse-tung, surrounded the city. The governor, Yang Hu-cheng, and General Li Hu-chen, known to the Chinese as the Two Tigers ("Hu"), were loyal to the Kuomintang. In such crises, missionaries and Chinese Christians, living in the suburbs outside the massive city walls, moved in for greater protection, but on this occasion fewer missionaries than usual were in Sian because of an annual conference being held in Hsingping. Englund and Roy Brehm, a new arrival in China, returning from the conference, were dismayed to find General Sung's army blocking their entry to Sian, but relieved to hear that missionaries trapped in the city were safe and well.

Englund saw the barred road to Sian as an opportunity for a week of tent evangelism in Lantien. On the way there, he was glad to find a Chinese Christian leader who also was alert to reap a harvest "out of season." The attacking army had dug trenches around the city walls, with one line extending to a small village where the church leader had his home. Hurriedly turning his house into a chapel, the elder led several officers and their men to Christ. With praise to God in his heart, Englund witnessed six of them being baptized. One was a former Moslem who later helped in getting messages in and out of the beleaguered city, but the siege had lasted long enough to make him anxious about Christians there and he determined to try and get them out. He was also concerned about funds which were getting critically low.

Negotiations with General Sung's command were tedious and long. Making a temporary home with Chinese Christians eight miles south of the city, Englund daily sloshed through deep mud and rain to the military headquarters. After agreement had been finally reached, Englund and Brehm crouched in a waterlogged trench on the appointed day, hopeful that missionaries and Chinese Christians would be set free, as promised. As they waited, Englund felt in his pocket and discovered that he was down to his last dollar. Guns were firing and bullets whistled overhead. Then the great city gate slowly opened, and a few Chinese came out, only to meet a fusillade which killed two and wounded others. The gate quickly closed again and a three day bombardment began. Englund once more visited army headquarters, trying to make himself heard above the roar of cannon and a bomb run by a lone plane. When the battle died down, contact was again made with those in the city, and Englund, accompanied by two English doctors and a missionary with a large red flag, crossed no man's land as resolutely as possible through knee-deep mud. Chinese and missionaries surged out of the city, and meeting them was "one of the most thrilling experiences" Englund ever had.

Among those to escape from the city was the Chinese manager of the Mission bookstore. His first question on meeting Englund was, "Do you need money?" Bullets flying in all directions were not an ideal background for a quiet discussion on financial problems, but Englund admitted that his funds were completely exhausted, and thankfully received hundreds of silver dollars hidden in the lining of the manager's coat. Business taken care of, they completed a safe crossing of no man's land.

Rescue for the missionaries had come none too soon. The siege lasted six and a half terrible months. The price of wheat rose to the equivalent of $50 (U.S.) a bushel, and 30,000 people were said to have perished. They were buried in two mass graves.

Sung Cheh-yuan's army was eventually driven off by General Feng Yu-hsiang, one of the most enigmatic figures on the North China scene, and known for a time as "the Christian general." He commanded a powerful Kuo-min-chun (People's) army, famous for its discipline and good behavior. Rain or shine, his troops marched in good order, singing hymns as they went. Officers and men attended church services whenever possible and gave generously to the poor. General Feng was originally a Moslem. After taking his stand as a Christian, he became a close friend of Jonathan Goforth, a man mightily used of God in Northeast China. When the general was governor of Shensi, he often visited The Evangelical Alliance Mission church and gave a message. But in 1926 he visited Russia and returned changed for the worse. His loyalty to the revolutionary cause of Sun Yat-sen was replaced by opposition to Chiang Kai-shek who defeated him in a Honan battle. More tragically, officers of his army who had once publicly praised God formed atheistic clubs and tried to outdo each other in blasphemy. They were perhaps following a trend to copy the French revolution of 1789.

The deliverance of Sian by General Feng was followed by significant changes. The city was renamed Hung-cheng, or Red City, and the old bell tower painted a corresponding color. Christians were shocked to see pegs driven into the walls of their churches, and horses tied to them. Students became arrogantly antichristian, and Feng's once Christian army made no effort to restrain them.

The rest of Shensi province remained in turmoil. For several weeks missionaries were under house arrest. Conferences planned for Sian and Lantien were canceled. Communist propaganda inspired by Soviet agents in Peking flooded Sian. Englund reported that a representative of the left wing of the Kuomintang had arrived to stir up bad feelings against missionaries and Chinese Christians. Antiforeign posters were put up all over the city and slanderous pamphlets distributed. Soldiers came and went, as the fortunes of internal wars ebbed and flowed. Departing troops took with them mules, horses, bulls and cows plundered from the villages, and retreating officers, perched precariously on piles of loot, were carried off by bullock carts, which they rode with as much dignity as if they had been in limousines.

In spite of chaotic conditions, the gospel continued to bear fruit and Englund's eyes were not on the red bell tower of Sian, but on the Cross of Calvary, where an irreversible victory had been won. Amid the swirl of cataclysmic events, his quiet trust in God was unshaken. "All is well with us" he wrote, "and we are safe in the Lord's hand in the midst of war storms and cannon thunder." Propaganda attacks on the church did not keep people from coming to Christ, even in the military. Two officers eager to give public witness to their new faith asked to be baptized. Preparations were made, but one of them received orders to move to another town on the very day of the service. Determined not to lose his opportunity, he pushed ahead with arrangements for the march so quickly that he salvaged a few free hours, ran all the way to the church, gave a radiant testimony to his faith in Christ and was baptized. Christians knelt in a circle around him, committing him to God's safekeeping and then away he went to lead his men to battle.

When Mr. and Mrs. Beckman left for furlough, care of the church inside the north gate of Sian was added to Englund's multiple responsibilities. His hope was that this would be only temporary and until "conference can do something about it, otherwise I'll be buried in all the work I have." He was feeling an acute need for someone to take care of household matters, but consoled himself with a mixture of faith and humor. "For one who is not good at cooking," he wrote, "there is not much time spent in preparing food, and besides, I'm taken up with Bible classes all day long. Today we have fasting and prayer. And so we forget all cooking responsibilities and let the Lord give richly of heavenly food."

Food was more easily forgotten than children. Miriam and Grace were still with Mr. and Mrs. Jacobsen in Changwu. Englund, who had not seen them for four months, sent a cart to bring them to Sian for Christmas. The journey which should have taken five days stretched out to two weeks. The people of Changwu had come to the limit of their patience and decided to resist any further demands from lawless troops who continually descended on them like a swarm of locusts. In revenge the soldiers joined up with the antiforeign Hard Bellies and surrounded the city. Englund also surrounded the city, with his prayers, believing with Elisha that the Lord's army of horses and chariots of fire is always superior to any force on earth. Christmas approached faster than the returning cart with his children and Englund had to leave for a Lantien conference without knowing how his prayers would be answered. But he could not have met with greater encouragement to believe that God always responds positively to persistent prayer.

The work and witness of the Lantien church had been seriously hindered by a smoldering quarrel between two elders, and by a bad relationship between one of the elders and his wife. For a year Englund had known and prayed about the situation. The Spirit of God began to move during the four days of conference. One evening the elder suddenly stood, but instead of attacking his fellow elder with bitter criticism, he broke into tears, confessing to God his own sin and failure. He went over to the old man, asking forgiveness, and then walking to the women's side of the church, made things right with his wife. For the senior elder it was perhaps harder, but in spite of his years, and losing face before the whole congregation, he in turn asked the younger brother's forgiveness. Now with hindrances washed away in tears of confession, God's blessing showered down on the church. With a beaming smile on his face, and a song in his heart, Englund praised God anew for hearing and answering prayer. Two days before Christmas, with a joyful and light step, Englund hurried back to Sian to find his children waiting, safe and well.

Peace on earth and goodwill toward men was hard to find at Christmas time 1926 in Northwest China. Christians meeting in the Sian church for a three day conference were reminded of the thunder of recent war by broken windows and holes in the ceiling. Special celebrations, planned for Christmas day, had to be abandoned when hostile students swarmed into the church determined to cause a disturbance. Violence increased the following day. Students and unarmed soldiers poured into the church, threw around the benches and pounded the floor as if they were demented. Failure to scare the Christians away infuriated them all the more. Englund's middle name, Gideon, was not given him in vain. Calling on Roy Brehm to blow mightily on his horn, he led the congregation in loud songs of praise. Down in the congregation, C. J. Jensen and Nils Jacobsen tried to keep some sort of order with the help of a diminutive but friendly policeman. "Keep singing, and use songs with the name of Jesus in them," Jensen shouted, and Englund and his trumpeter responded magnificently. "Silent Night" was obviously not appropriate to the occasion. For an hour the tumult continued. Students and soldiers screamed blasphemy, Brehm blew his trumpet, Englund encouraged the congregation and Christians joyfully sang the praises of Jesus Christ and His saving power, until victory was theirs.

A long antichristian demonstration in the church yard delayed a baptismal service, but did not frighten 14 men and women from publicly professing their faith the following day. Even the new provincial governor, General Feng Yu-hsiang, who had raised the siege of Sian, sent two officers to apologize for the disturbance and promised that it would not be repeated. The Governor's Christian testimony, tarnished by a visit to the U.S.S.R., had not completely disappeared. Although the provincial government was largely communistic and had direct connections with ten Russian advisors, General Feng kept a close check on extreme radicals and always had a friendly welcome for Englund and other missionaries who sought audience with him. He personally wrote a letter to a group of English Baptists, enclosing permits for their return to Shensi, and expressed satisfaction at their coming. And General Chang Chih-chiang, known as the Moody of Feng's once Christian army, was said to be as wholehearted for Christ as ever and in line for an important post over Shensi and Kansu provinces. But the flag of the new Chinese Republic was hauled down, and the red flag of revolution flew over the city. Even more radical in Chinese eyes, women were given equal rights with men, and to the utter amazement of traditionalists, a woman was elected magistrate. Those who had memories of the formidable Manchu Dowager Empress, often called "Old Buddha," trembled in their shoes.

Yet another dark shadow was creeping remorselessly toward the agonized Northwest. Incessant fighting had destroyed countless homes and left the countryside stark and barren. A dry fall was followed by a cold, bleak winter. Food shortages reduced everyone to a common level more quickly than any social revolution. Shivering, starving, homeless people pulled their rags around them as they huddled in the ruins of war, the wealthy hardly any better off than the poorest. Christians, with no special immunity from these calamities, at least had the sustaining and sure hope that in the City to which they were journeying they would "hunger no more, neither thirst any more; neither shall the sun strike upon them, nor any heat; for the Lamb that is in the midst of the throne shall be their shepherd, and shall guide them unto fountains of waters of life; and God shall wipe every tear from their eyes." As Englund said at the time, "The gloomy atmosphere had its effect on gospel work, but the grace of God is sufficient also for this."

To the desolation of war and famine, and the turmoil of continuing revolution, was added another ugly problem. Englund understood well Paul's experience in Macedonia, where he was "afflicted on every side; without were fightings, within were fears." The fears were not personal, but for the church. The revolutionary spirit of the age infected some of its workers. Forgetting that in Christ there is neither "Jew nor Greek," Chinese nor foreigner, they were more zealous for change and freedom than for the unity of all true believers. A few of the more arrogant were reluctantly dismissed from their responsibilities, and found balm for their hurt feelings by joining with the leader of an independent movement, ambitious to grow rapidly by swallowing the long established church on the north side of Sian.

Any slight hope that peace might come at last to the province was roughly shattered in 1927 when communist propaganda and antichristian activity exploded all over China. Sian was the center of the movement and once again all missionaries were ordered to the Coast where the International Settlement of Shanghai offered relative security. Englund, now leader of all TEAM work in Shensi province, tired but still confident in God, returned with his daughters to the United States for furlough. His hearing had become distressingly worse. The nerve system was deteriorating rapidly and even a long and cumbersome ear trumpet was not much help. For the rest of his life he would never enjoy ideal conditions for his ministry.

8

Bible School Principal

Anna Johansen sailed out of San Francisco one December day in 1921 fully confident that God had called her to China. She could remember William Englund, home on furlough, telling thrilling stories of Lantien and Sian, when he spoke to the Sunday school and preached in the Vroom Street Evangelical Free Church in Jersey City. She smiled as she recalled his Chinese clothes, slight bow at the end of his message and short steps as he walked back to his chair.

Anna had early connections with China. Her cousin, Herman Swenson, had been there since 1912, accompanying Englund on some of his pioneer trips. Swenson and Englund had often laughed over an incident which was funnier in retrospect than at the time. They had spent a night in a bug-ridden inn where sleep was nearly impossible. Swenson patiently attacked the enemy, giving Englund a running commentary on the course of the battle. Then Englund began to give a report on developments in his area and suddenly called out, "Herman, I have something here much bigger than a louse!" Joint investigations revealed that his prisoner was a mouse which had crawled up his pajama leg.

Swenson had written from China suggesting that Anna contact Mr. and Mrs. Ahlstrand and travel out with them when their furlough ended. But he gave no contact address and mission records were rather casual in those days. God, however, keeps a daily watch over the movements of His servants and directs their steps. Anna and her roommate were riding the Brooklyn subway on their way to a speaking engagement. The girl was carrying a Bible which attracted the attention of a woman standing next to her. A conversation began and Anna and her friend found that they were talking to Mrs. Ahlstrand.

Commissioned in the Vroom Street Free Church for missionary service, Anna joined the Ahlstrands when they returned to China. Christmas was celebrated aboard ship. A week later Shanghai welcomed them with cheerful confusion. The long journey to Shensi province followed, first by river steamer to Hankow and from there by train to the end of the line. Mule litter was normal transportation for the final section of travel, but on this occasion horsepower broke the mule monopoly. General Feng Yu-hsiang had sent a car from Sian to pick up a YMCA official and party. When the car broke down, the indomitable general dispatched a second vehicle and the first car, after being repaired, was available for the Ahlstrands and Anna Johansen, who thus became the first missionaries to arrive in Sian by car. They lost count of how many reckless dogs they accidentally killed along the way.

General Feng had another courtesy to offer. He invited all missionaries to a reception for the YMCA director and meeting Anna for the first time, asked Swenson what her Chinese name was. When the general learned that she had just arrived and had not been given a name, he said, "Then I will choose one for her. It shall be Chan Tien-an (Heaven's Peace)."

For language study, Anna lived with her cousins, Mr. and Mrs. Swenson, in Kuyuan, Kansu province. But before she could learn anything from the Chinese she repeatedly had to answer their questions about the secret of her soft, golden hair. Women in particular were always asking, "What do you eat to make it that color?"

Much of Kuyuan had been destroyed in the devastating earthquake of 1920 which rocked Kansu. Two years later great crevasses could still be seen where men and animals had been instantly swallowed up alive. Swenson, daring the fury of a Moslem reaction, pioneered there. Superstition and opposition broke before the hammer blows of God's Word and by the second year 23 men and women had been baptized. Anna soon began to put her newly acquired language to good use, working among women and children and visiting in homes. Official opposition to the gospel was gradually worn down by kindness, which was demonstrated in a special way when missionaries supplied food to hundreds of people during a 23-day siege of the city by a horde of bloodthirsty bandits. But the same nationwide antiforeign movement which forced William Englund in 1927 out of Shensi to Shanghai and home, took Anna Johansen out of Kansu and back to the United States. In September of that year, the Rev. Thorvald Johansen, a missionary of The Evangelical Alliance Mission on furlough from India, united them in marriage. Ahead of them lay 42 years of happiness and fruitful service in many lands.

Rev. and Mrs. Englund crossed the Pacific aboard the Japanese SS Korea Maru in December 1928, and for the second time Anna celebrated Christmas at sea. *Celebrate* is rather a misleading word to describe that particular occasion. In spite of a raging storm, some passengers managed to attend a service at which Englund preached, but his wife was missing from the congregation. "Her loss has surely been the fish's gain," he wrote. Changing ship in Japan, the Englunds traveled to Chefoo, Shantung province, where the China Inland Mission had a large school for missionary children. As their own Mission at that time was not able to arrange for the education of children in the disturbed Northwest, Englund and his wife had no choice but to leave Miriam and Grace in the Chefoo school. Only God and parents know the hurt of separation from much loved children, a pain that lingers unrelieved until the day of exhuberant reunion.

The route to Sian was familiar, but the city had a new face, harsh and unfriendly. Its name had been changed to New City. Carts rumbled out with loads of stone blocks from the old streets in preparation for building smooth motor roads. Even parts of the massive gates, which for centuries had withstood many an assault, were torn down for the sake of the all-conquering automobile. Trees were being planted everywhere, but not all improvements had a peaceful purpose. Englund noticed that an unused mill had been converted into an ammunition factory. "Plowshares are still being beaten into swords," he reported to his home church, "and we have to wait until the Lord orders swords to be made over to plows." The reason for war preparations soon became obvious. Chiang Kai-shek had learned a great deal about communism during his time in Moscow. After accepting help from Chinese communists in his campaign against the Northern warlords in 1926, he decided that the short-lived marriage between the left and right wing parties of the Kuomintang must end. Separation became a fact the following year and the Generalissimo's unwavering policy crystalized into a plan for the complete destruction of all communist forces in China. Military leaders in Sian, with their strong addiction to the Soviet camp, prepared for battle.

Not only war threatened to bring death and destruction once more to the unhappy North. Famine stalked through the land. Fields had turned into deserts. Men were selling their wives and daughters in a final, desperate effort to get money for food, expensive beyond all reason. Others pulled down their houses to burn as fuel until the inevitable day arrived when they sat cold and starving on the ashes of what had been their home.

William and Anna Englund, walking the country roads, were horrified to see farmers reduced to "bony human shadows with deep-sunken eyes glaring listlessly out of their sockets. Others had given up the struggle and laid down by the roadside for their final sleep." Poor, bleeding China was dying of hunger and thirst, physical and spiritual. Missionaries dreaded the helpless agony of leaving their homes to walk through crowded lanes where skeleton hands of dying men and women clutched at them, pleading for help. Famine relief was generously given, but pitifully small in comparison with the sea of need. Only Jesus Himself, multiplying bread and fish, from dawn to weary dusk, could have turned the tide of starvation.

When Englund and his fellow missionaries met in the Sian Church for their annual spring conference in 1929, it brought back stirring memories, for here he and Brehm had trumpeted and sung their way to victory three years before. Famine still prevailed and meat was unobtainable. Mr. and Mrs. Jacobson, responsible for feeding 29 people for the ten days of conference, had bought up as many chickens as they could find and soon disappeared in a flurry of feathers as they prepared meals. One of the important decisions of the conference was to open a Bible institute. Pioneer evangelism and church outreach no longer depended entirely on missionary effort. God had given rich gifts to His church in China and a place of training was urgently needed. Chaotic conditions, which had forced the closing down of the Sian Seminary, had not noticeably improved, but Englund and others had learned that to wait for ideal circumstances would be to wait forever. With faith stretched to the limit, they prayed that at least eight students would register for the new Bible Institute, paying their own expenses. Mr. and Mrs. William Englund were asked to accept responsibility for the school.

Englund himself had overcome the handicap of not attending Bible school or seminary by a diligent, systematic and personal study of the Scriptures with the Holy Spirit as his tutor. He taught himself Latin and Greek and acquired the habit of using a Greek New Testament in his early morning devotions. Combined with a wide and practical knowledge of the Word of God, he was ready for the classroom. His objective was clear. He would give himself to teaching young Chinese the glories of Christ as revealed in Scripture so that, with burning hearts, they would make Him known for the salvation of the lost and the maturing of believers. His method was equally simple. By word in the classroom, by example in evangelism, and by life at all times, he would teach and demonstrate the truth.

Expectantly, Englund waited in the new Bible Institute for students to enroll. The first to arrive was a young man from the mountains. The people of his village had tried to stop him by tying his hands together and stringing him up to a beam, with the intention of thrashing him until he gave up his faith in Christ. But every time they hoisted him to the beam, the rope broke, and they let him go. However, other enemies were waiting for him on the lonely road to Sian. Armed bandits accosted him and split his throat open with a spear. Bloody but determined, he continued on his way to the Institute where his wounds were taken care of and he was enrolled. He was not the most brilliant of students. Being conscious that his first efforts in an examination were not very good, he added an apology for the inadequate answers, "My paper may not rate any high marks, but the spiritual lessons and blessings I take in are fully one hundred per cent."

God had more than answered the prayer for eight students. A Chinese teacher, Mr. Hsieh, had come to help and in the classroom were 18 enthusiastic young men. None of them had attained the heights of China's scholar class by passing an examination for the coveted "hsiu-tsai" (B.A.) degree. Men of learning had been won for Christ and were serving Him with outstanding ability, but scholars reasoned that since they were already trained to study they could apply themselves to the Scriptures without attending a Bible institute or seminary. It was almost impossible to persuade them differently.

Students soon found that the Institute was not an academic sanctuary, but a place of meeting with God in preparation for meeting with men. On Englund's suggestion teachers and students set aside a full day for prayer and fasting. As they waited quietly before God, the Holy Spirit began moving among them like a strong breeze stirring the trees at evening. Sins ignored or covered up with alibis were brought to light and confessed and the students, overwhelmed by God's presence, learned that He needed to work in them before He could work through them. "I feel as though I had become a believer all over again since coming here," exclaimed one of them. The reality of his fresh meeting with God was proved when he visited the Lantien church for a series of special services. He began by following the example of Englund, spending the first day in prayer and fasting. One of the church elders then joined him in the fields where they pleaded with God for blessing in abundance. As they prayed together, a young man came along to ask what they were doing. When he heard, he said, "Then please pray for me too. I want to be saved," and falling on his knees he accepted Christ. Blessing in the church followed. Sleeping Christians were aroused and sinners brought to Christ. Even on the journey back to Sian, the student was used of God to lead four people to the Savior.

Other students also became on fire for God. Almost every afternoon the Bible Institute emptied of teachers and students as they fanned out into the city streets and nearby villages, preaching as they went. Englund was often in the lead, his zeal inspiring the students to organize evangelistic teams to pioneer in remote and dark areas. The Bible Institute was something more than a school, it was an experience. God was multiplying the ministry of William Englund by bringing to him young men who would catch his compassion for lost people and go like torchbearers to all parts of the suffering land.

Even with full time responsibility for the Bible Institute, Englund somehow managed to sandwich in visits to a few churches for Bible conferences. He responded to an invitation to spend nine days in

Kienhsien where over 20,000 people had died of starvation. The windows of the church, all smashed during an antichristian demonstration, were open to bitter December winds. Food was still terribly scarce, but Christians cheerfully endured all hardships and met four times a day to enjoy God's Word. Even women, who had great difficulty in leaving their daily chores, numbered 200. People coming from a distance had been promised lodging in side rooms of the church, but as Englund stood to preach at an afternoon session, he was told that soldiers had arrived and were demanding use of the premises. He went to talk with the officer in charge, but before he could say more than a word or two, the man retorted, "The Bible says, 'If any man take away thy coat, let him have thy cloak also,' and you will not even make room for us in the church." The officer emphasized his rather unusual interpretation of Scripture by ordering his troops to bring in their artillery, rifles and horses. He was considerate enough to leave the conference meetings undisturbed, but Christian women from the country had to manage as best they could for sleeping quarters.

The Bible-quoting officer used Scripture to his maximum advantage, whether talking to Christians or unbelievers, and when the Englunds prepared to leave Kienhsien they found that every animal, cart and Chinese wheelbarrow had been confiscated. A sympathetic farmer eventually produced two antiques, whose only link with their original state was a wobbly wheel roughly held in place by old planks. One contraption carried the baggage; the other William and Anna Englund. But sitting cross-legged, Chinese style, proved more uncomfortable than walking. As they trudged along, Englund was forced to master a new trade in a hurry. His wife lost a heel from one of her shoes. The only tools available were a couple of large stones, and with this primitive equipment William banged the heel into place while Anna patiently stood on one foot for a "repair while you wait" job. The cobbler's work was done to the customer's satisfaction and "so substantially as to keep the heel there ever since," he wrote triumphantly.

A conference at Hsingping was also well attended in spite of the terrible winter. Between 700 and 800 people gathered daily, not only to have their own spiritual needs met, but also to prepare for reaching dying multitudes with the gospel. The famine had not abated and many a pastor on Sundays was facing a congregation whose faces had turned black with hunger.

Englund's total commitment to giving out the Word of God is vividly highlighted in a letter he wrote on his return to Sian after the Hsingping conference. "We have just returned from our trip," he wrote. "A touch of influenza put me in bed a couple of days. At noon the next day two rickshaws were waiting outside our door to take us fifteen miles out in the country for three days of meeting at a big market town." Englund watched with amusement as his traveling companion, Rev. K. B. Vatsaas, settled himself into a vehicle, which, even in its youth, was never designed for a man of his bulk. The old wheels changed from being approximately circular to definitely oval, and as they bumped over the rough country roads, the tires grew thin and flat from want of air, while the heroic coolie puffed and blew as if he had an excess of what the tires lacked. Relief arrived in the form of a large farm cart, drawn by a team of mules. Vatsaas thankfully transferred himself and his baggage to the more adequate form of transportation, while the rickshaw man, equally thankful, turned around and dragged his ancient vehicle back to Sian before the crooked wheels collapsed completely.

As Englund crossed the narrow stone bridge leading to the town, famous stories and old memories came to mind. The famous emperor Chin Shih Huang, builder of the Great Wall, had often been carried over the bridge in his imperial sedan chair, accompanied by innumerable courtiers. The bridge had never been widened for carts, and when Englund and Roy Brehm had brought refugees from the besieged city of Sian a few years earlier their mule and cart had been forced to ford the swift and swollen river. Englund remembered standing on the bridge praying for the animal as it was swept away down stream by the rushing waters. The mule may not have known why its life was spared that day, but Englund knew and thanked God. This time the only animals making the trip were what Englund called his "dairy," a faithful cow and its calf. A venomous scorpion, coiled up under Englund's bedding all the time he was in town, was not an official member of the party, but was kept in check by the watch-care of God.

Englund shared with the local Christians six messages on the triumphs of faith recorded in Hebrews 11. Christians of the Northwest had firsthand experience of "the edge of the sword, the power of fire, mockings, being destitute, afflicted and ill treated," and as the conference progressed they had a fresh experience of God's grace to sustain even amidst the miseries of famine, cold and snow.

9

Priorities and Pressure

All through his long ministry on the China mainland, Englund faced two major problems. One was to strike a proper balance between his varied activities and the other was to discern God's will through the crowding pressure of daily events. Towards the end of 1930 both problems came to a simultaneous climax. His first responsibility was the Sian Bible Institute. He was also treasurer for his own Mission and other evangelistic societies working in the Northwest, and he was frequently invited to speak at conferences which usually lasted several days. Nevertheless, he always cared for his responsibilities as a husband and a father. Bible teaching, Mission business and family affairs were usually taken care of amid the swirl of China's military and political turbulence. Daily pressures often determined his activities but never diminished his dependence on God.

That year the armies of Chiang Kai-shek were preparing to sweep north in a bloody campaign that would cost a quarter of a million casualties, killed and wounded. In Shensi province, as rebellious generals braced for battle, William and Anna Englund eagerly awaited a happier event, the birth of their first child. Missionary forces of The Evangelical Alliance Mission had been sadly reduced that year by eight deaths, including a little child, but reinforcements were arriving, among them eight new workers, born of missionary parents in China. One of them was Thyra Beckman whose mother and two sisters had laid down their lives for Christ in the terrible massacre in 1911. Finally there was the arrival of a baby girl, Winifred, to bring joy to William Englund and his wife. She was dedicated on Christmas day, 1930 at a simple service in the home of Mr. and Mrs. Vatsaas and almost immediately introduced to the humor and hardship of missionary travel.

The Bible Institute's winter recess freed the Englunds for their first vacation in two busy years. They spent 20 days of it traveling by cart from Sian to Kuyuan, in the neighboring province of Kansu, to celebrate with their fellow missionaries the 40th anniversary of the arrival of the first TEAM workers in China. Baby Winifred traveled snugly in a basket slung from the cart in which her parents rode, their feet wrapped in heavy bearskins as protection from snow and storm. Englund surveyed the arrangements with satisfaction. "The disciples let Paul down in a basket, but we have our baby hung up in one," he remarked. Then as the party approached Chingchuan at dusk he no longer trusted the precious burden to slithering mules and cart. Calling on his fellow missionary, Julius Bergstrom, for help, he tied the basket to a long coolie pole, which the two men shouldered along the dark and slippery road until soldiers halted them at the city gates. The officer in charge insisted on a thorough search of baggage and baby in spite of the intense cold and late hour. "I'm not here to take care of babies," he growled, "I'm a soldier."

Other missionaries had rougher treatment. Soldiers looted the town where Miss Anna Skollenberg was living and after beating her and cutting her arm, left her with no outer clothes or bedding. She wrapped herself in wadded door curtains and awaited rescue. Nevertheless, sufferings, dangers and difficulties were eclipsed by a review of four decades of blessing. War, drought, famine, revolution and disease had ebbed and flowed across the unhappy land, but the gates of hell had not prevailed. Thousands of people had turned to Christ. Churches had been established. Even priests, saturated with the vague doctrines of Buddhism or lost in the mysteries of Taoism, had been delivered from the power of darkness and brought into the kingdom of God's dear Son. The fires of revival had not been extinguished and an increasing number of Chinese men and women were being trained to witness effectively for Christ. God's power and glory were being revealed and so they sang together, those missionaries in conference, rejoicing in what God had done and expecting yet greater things. It was for this that they prayed. Although Englund was one in heart with them, he had great difficulty in hearing the prayers of others. Even his ear trumpet failed to make conversation audible. The day was slowly approaching when the only voice William Englund would ever hear would be that of God Himself.

Conference ended just in time. The morning after the missionaries left Kuyuan, trouble broke out in the city. The military commander had strengthened his forces by incorporating into his army a large band of brigands who had fled from Shensi province. Their warlike qualities were more reliable than their promises, and having been welcomed into Kuyuan in good faith by their new commander, they responded by throwing the old gentleman into jail, looting the city and disarming the original army.

Back in Sian, the Englunds faced new difficulties. General Feng Yu-hsiang's career as a soldier was following the pattern of his life as a Christian. Spiritual defeat after his visit to Russia was a prelude to defeat on the battlefield. He had thrown in his lot with Wang Ching-wei, who had set up a new "National Government" in Peking in opposition to Chiang Kai-shek. The Generalissimo, in a victorious march north, was about to emerge as the supreme ruler of all China. His forces penetrated Shensi province. Sian was bombed and once more the city braced itself for a siege. Provincial paper money lost all value, and life itself was not worth much more. Local troops and militia impetuously sought safety in flight, sneaking out of the city by night. In a desperate rush, men killed their families to make escape easier, but moments later were themselves swept to death by the surging current of the Wei River. The city gates were closed against the approaching armies, sealing up the citizens to their uncertain fate. With no one to keep order, looters greedily saw a golden opportunity to take advantage of the general panic, but were thwarted by the prayers of God's people. Englund and his fellow missionaries had been sleeping with their clothes on, ready to run if danger came too close, but a sudden, heavy rainstorm kept even the most villainous robber off the streets. God's Word was a source of immense strength in those days, and Englund held tightly to the promise that "a man shall be as a hiding place from the wind and a covert from the tempest; as rivers of water in a dry place, as the shadow of a great rock in a weary land."

The first sentences of three consecutive paragraphs of a letter written during those violent and tragic days are in amazing contrast to the local turmoil. "Our Bible school work has suffered no interruption . . .. It has been a joyful privilege to take part in some special meetings again here and there . . .. It was a time of spiritual refreshing," Englund wrote. It was as if he was living in another world and indeed he was.

God's promises were speedily made good and a short period of unusual peace came to the Northwest, accelerating Englund's activities. Through the witness of the Bible school students and teachers, churches were established in the village homes of new believers. Englund himself was able to get back to Lantien for a quick visit. His old house had been burned down and soldiers still occupied all the church premises except the auditorium. Hundreds of Christians poured in from the countryside for four days of special meetings, undeterred by news that the city had been the scene of bitter fighting when bandit forces attacked. Several women came 30 miles on foot, bringing a new believer with whom they enjoyed three days of good fellowship along the way. Englund had feared that endless troubles and suffering might have caused "the holy fire to burn low on the altars of some hearts," and as a precaution took "two firebrands" from the Bible school with him. The precaution was neither entirely necessary, nor in vain. Their passion for Christ stirred others and when night fell, Englund, in a tiny makeshift room beside the pulpit, thanked God that the windows of heaven are always open to pour down blessings.

A little later in that same year, 1931, the Lantien church was free of its military squatters, and able to open a refugee camp for over 300 women and children threatened by a terrible famine that held the Northwest in its deadly grip. Food and Bible teaching were provided daily; the former limited by supplies on hand, the latter in unlimited quantities. As a test a long row of boys was lined up in the church one day and asked to repeat in unison memorized Scriptures. They kept going as fast as words could flow for almost half an hour and even then had not finished all they knew.

The Hsingping church also eagerly seized the opportunity of the strangely quiet months. Arriving as conference speaker, Englund found the largest gathering of Christians ever seen in the city. Solomon Bergstrom had prayed, wept, worked and preached in the area for more than 25 years, and as he lay dying in 1929, could thank God for more than 2,000 men and women who had come to know Jesus Christ as Savior and Lord. There were at least 2,000 more registered as serious inquirers and a total of 11 churches and 13 preaching points in the district. The Hsingping church building proved too small for the crowds that poured into the city, hungry for the Word of God and hopeful of help in the misery of famine. A big tent was hurriedly erected to take the overflow and filled immediately. Night after night Englund and some of the Bible school students preached at crowded services and saw men and women transformed by a new revival. The return journey to Sian was in the luxury of an overloaded Mission bus driven by Julius Bergstrom. Mule carts were losing their long monopoly; missionaries were losing familiar aches in their joints.

After three days of what Englund called "crowded and very blessed meetings at the west station church in Sian," a dream came true. For two and a half years the Englunds had not seen their daughters, Miriam and Grace. Constant war had made travel to Chefoo almost impossible, but at last the roads were safe. The new bus cut down travel time from Sian to the railhead from one week to one day, and when the Englunds arrived in Peking three and a half days after leaving home, they had broken all mission records for speed. After the shortest possible stop for optical and dental needs they hurried on to Tientsin by train, and then by ship to Chefoo. For the whole summer in a house half way up a hill and with a magnificent view of the ocean, they enjoyed what they needed and longed for: family life with all three children. But before the vacation could be enjoyed, Englund had to dispose of a familiar enemy. Scorpions were peculiarily attracted to him, always to their disadvantage. The hillside house was full of them and after the first battle thirty lay dead. A counterattack began the following morning when a lone patrol came crawling down the corner of the bedroom as Englund awoke. The only weapon at hand was his Bible, which he wielded with deadly effect. As he shared with his family at breakfast the story of another victory, he concluded with his usual big smile, "And it reminded me that the Bible is always our best weapon against the Evil One."

Daily blessings that quiet summer in Chefoo were as regular as sunrise. With his strong imagination, Englund could tell a Bible story as vividly as if he had personally witnessed the event. His children never forgot. Every day came to a happy conclusion with a graphic account of David adventuring with God, Daniel fearlessly facing kings and lions, or Moses challenging the terrible Pharaoh in the name of the great I AM. Miriam and Grace were old enough to know the meaning of a personal faith in Christ and to trust Him confidently as Savior. As the Bible story ended, William and Anna listened with joyful and thankful hearts to their two little girls praying to a heavenly Father known and loved.

Summer in Chefoo was intended as a time of rest. But let Englund himself describe it. "First I helped in five days of Bible classes at the Presbyterian Mission. Then followed eight days of special meetings at the China Inland Mission Chinese Church. The presence and blessing of the Lord were truly remarkable in all these gatherings. We also took part in the evangelistic work among U.S. Marines, besides preaching here and there as we were invited. My dear wife had the girls' needs to attend to in addition to being my faithful helper in the treasurer's work of the Mission."

The weeks sped by at what seemed twice the normal rate and like clouds darkening a sunny landscape, the inevitable day of separation approached remorselessly. Good food lost its taste, family prayers were punctuated by tears and a favorite Bible story was told for the last time. Prolonged goodnight kisses were a desperate attempt to stop time from moving on, but nothing could delay the unwelcome day when Miriam and Grace returned to school, and their parents, with little Winifred, once more turned their faces towards Sian. The girls had to shout their "good-bys." William Englund was now very deaf.

The happy, peaceful summer had ended, and Sian Bible Institute urgently needed their principal back for a fall term which had already begun with temporary help from Rev. Julius Bergstrom and his mother . . . but unexpected problems again interfered with travel. A bomb explosion on the South Manchurian Railway tracks in 1931 gave the Japanese a flimsy excuse for seizing Mukden with their Kwantung army as a "self defense" move. Chiang Kai-shek's troops were tied down in a determined campaign to exterminate communist forces, and handicapped by a devastating Yangtze River flood which had left two million dead, countless people homeless and a sea of mud. In the words of Englund, "the big war was getting nearer our doors," but no one then realized how terrible the conflict would become.

The doctor treating Mrs. Englund in Chefoo had suggested an examination by a specialist at the famed Peking Union Medical College hospital. A delay of a day or two on the way back to Sian did not seem unreasonable, but when the specialist advised an immediate operation, Englund faced the problem of listening to medical counsel or responding to an urgent need at the Bible Institute. A baby, less than a year old, added to the difficulty. As usual in such times of uncertainty, he "turned to the Lord in prayer and it became clear to us." Anna Englund entered the hospital. William Englund and his little daughter were given a warm welcome at the Home of Rest where Mr. and Mrs. Kok of the Netherlands Legation had found a way to serve the Lord outside their official duties. Mr. Kok also took advantage of long summer vacations by riding a donkey from village to village, preaching the gospel as he went.

While Anna recovered from a successful operation, her husband was busy teaching the Scriptures in Peking churches, and soon, rejoicing over fresh experiences of the presence and help of the Lord, the family was ready to continue on their way to Sian. After long experience with wheelbarrows, mule carts, bicycles and trucks, Englund was so well conditioned to China travel that he wrote to friends in the U.S. that he and his wife had "no trouble" on their journey home. On the train out of Peking they had a comfortable sleeping compartment, but one meal in the diner was sufficient to keep them from eating there for the rest of the trip. A change at Chengchow gave them a full day of rest in the home of the Free Methodist missionaries, but at Loyang, where a change of trains was necessary, the only accomodation was the local inn. Guests were expected to provide their own bedding and the Englunds were dismayed to learn that none of their checked baggage had traveled with them. They spent the night on a wooden bed covered with one borrowed blanket. Two days later the missing bedding arrived and the journey resumed to Lingpao where Mr. Vatsaas had patiently waited with a car until the morning of the third day. Unfortunately he returned to Sian shortly before the Englund's train arrived. They finished their "trouble free" journey on a truck of the International Famine Relief.

Sian began to feel a fresh impact from the Bible Institute when a preaching chapel, or "life saving station" as Englund called it, was opened on the main street. Electricity and sophisticated entertainment had not reached the Northwest and the main pleasures in leisure hours were eating, tea drinking and an occasional Chinese opera. Enthusiastic Christians had little difficulty in persuading merchants, students, soldiers and others with time to spare to turn off the busy street into the chapel and listen to the "happy sound" of the gospel.

Evening by evening, Bible school teachers (often including Englund) and students, witnessed one after another to the power of Christ to save. Proud scholars, fanatical Moslems, untaught coolies, illiterate farmers, people of all classes heard, believed and entered into life.

As January, 1932 came to a close, Englund had many reasons to be thankful to God. In spite of war, famine, disease and personal difficulties, he was seeing the first ten men graduate from the Institute, prepared for full time Christian service. He also had an encouraging reminder of God's power to keep. In his early years in China, Englund had unhappily watched a Christian girl from the Mission school being sent away by her parents to marry an unbeliever. The red bridal chair and silk gown had proved false omens of a happy married life. Seventeen years of pagan pressures, daily persecution, increasing tragedy and sorrow had passed over the girl and brought her back to Englund's front door, a half-blind widow. Her faith had not failed and she had come a long day's journey to express her thanks for being led to Christ in childhood.

Englund managed to keep a delicate balance between his responsibilities as principal of the Bible Institute and opportunities as a conference speaker. Lantien, Hsingping, Pucheng, Huhsien and other churches were always in his prayers, and when spring came, his feet followed his heart. As usual, the Hsingping church was overcrowded and Englund had the double problem of speaking loud enough to reach more than a hundred people listening outside the building through an open window, and overcoming the handicap of a bad cold.

Travel in Shensi was speeding up. Distances were shrinking and new discomforts emerging. Dust raised by the old mule carts was nothing compared to what automobiles could do. At the end of long journeys passengers were all one earthy brown color, regardless of race. The ride back to Sian aggravated Englund's cold, forcing him to abandon plans to visit his beloved Lantien. Pastor Kuo, who took his place, reported that blessing was as abundant as the drenching rains, and as overwhelming as the flooding rivers. But Englund's cold did not keep him out of action long and even before Pastor Kuo returned to Sian, he climbed aboard a truck heading for Pucheng where the Swedish Mission in China worked. Like other passengers, his only seat was on the baggage. At every stop, bedding rolls, often not very clean, were hurled onto the truck and were followed by their owners who sat wherever the rolls landed. Englund, in his little corner, was at times almost buried by the barrage of bedrolls, and glad for an occasional breath of fresh air when all passengers were ordered off the truck to add manpower to insufficient horsepower up steep and muddy hills. The only obvious benefit of this new means of travel was that the journey was reduced from three days to one. A reward for discomfort was to see God's blessing fall on the church far more abundantly than bedrolls on the truck.

Englund reverted to the less spectacular mule cart for his trip to Huhsien, a city with a history going back over 3,000 years. On an artificial mound surrounded by an earth wall he found a large stone with a carved inscription identifying it as the public platform of the first emperor of the great Chou dynasty (B.C. 1122). A Buddhist priest and an angry dog discouraged Englund from close investigation of the site and from occupying the imperial pulpit. Instead he chose to speak four times a day in a little street chapel, which was far too small for the occasion.

As Englund returned to Sian, famine, disease and violence began again to march through the land. Gustaf Tornvall, born in China of missionary parents, was murdered by bandit soldiers on his way to the city bringing famine relief funds. For 18 months Englund, as Field Treasurer, had eagerly checked quarterly transmissions from the home office in the hope of finding support promised by Tornvall's church, but depression was strangling the American economy and many Christians were having serious financial difficulties. A private legacy, said to be on the way, had not arrived. For six months Tornvall had gently refused to be a burden on his fellow missionaries or hinder the work of the gospel by accepting help from general field funds, even as a loan. Englund finally persuaded him to accept an advance grant of support, but when the long expected check arrived, Tornvall was already with Christ, and as Englund opened his ledger to close the personal account, he could not see the page for tears.

Death, like a hungry giant, terrorized the province. Within a few months cholera had carried 100,000 people swiftly to their graves. Failure of the wheat harvest also threatened those who had escaped sudden death by disease with slower death by starvation. For missionaries there was the extra threat of death by violence. No one leaving home could be sure of returning. The old Chinese proverb, "A thousand days at home are good, but step out of the door and troubles begin," took on a grim and sinister meaning. The Englunds never imagined that a young Pentecostal missionary whom they had invited to supper and wished Godspeed on his journey to Kansu province would be shot dead before he had traveled many miles, but for all who "sat in the shadow of death," the Bible Institute teachers and students had good news. Crowds listened as Englund and others preached through the entire Epistle to the Romans, verse by verse. "As sin reigned in death, even so might grace reign through righteousness unto eternal life through Jesus Christ our Lord," was certainly a relevant message to dying people.

An inevitable counterattack followed. The Nationalist Party Headquarters local newspaper complained that Christian preaching was being carried on in Sian more than ever in spite of repeated efforts to crush it and called on the provincial authorities to prohibit further evangelism. When nothing came of the protest, the newspaper saved face by inserting a notice saying that representatives had been sent to all places where the gospel was being preached and promises were received that in the future no one would be forced to attend Christian services. Englund, knowing that no reporter had visited any church, laughed and prayed that the book of Acts might be brought up to date to read, "Did we not straitly command you that you should not teach in this Name and, behold, you have filled Sian with your doctrine."

Englund made up for missing a visit to Lantien earlier in the year by going there for special meetings at a time of a terrible cholera epidemic. Thousands died as fast as graves could be dug, but very few Christians were struck down. One Lantien elder likened it to the immunity enjoyed by Israel when God blasted Egypt with devastating plagues. Great numbers gathered for the conference and were not disappointed. Christians were revived and unbelievers brought to Christ. Englund, looking over a radiant and animated congregation, and thinking of hostility and death all around like storm waves dashing against a rock, suddenly recalled words spoken of Stephen as he faced martyrdom: "He, being full of the Holy Spirit, looked up stedfastly into Heaven." A few days later in a letter to the home office he wrote, "Praise be to God for that same upward look regardless of what earthly conditions and outlook may be."

The normal, robust health of Englund now declined. His ministry as Field Treasurer, Bible School superintendent and teacher, conference speaker and evangelist was demanding more strength than he had. At times he could not leave his bed. Doctors suspected that his appendix might be the problem and recommended an operation in Shanghai. With famine and cholera making it impossible to enroll a new class at the Bible Institute, Englund felt that he could make the trip to the coast without putting too heavy a load on the rest of the staff. The operation was more complicated than expected and the effects of the anesthetic almost worse than the original symptoms. On Thanksgiving Day, 1932 Anna was able to praise God for a successful operation on her husband, but for William there were two months of violent headaches every time he tried to sit up. Yet wrapped in the trial was a blessing. Miriam and Grace, who would not have been able to spend Christmas vacation in Sian because of a fresh outbreak of communistic activity there, were reunited with their parents in Shanghai.

Reports from the Northwest were a chilling reminder that peace on earth was as rare as men of goodwill. A radiogram brought news that all Shensi missionaries had been called into the relative safety of Sian city because of new communist troop movements. What action the city governor would take and where his loyalty lay was unknown. Another distressing report was of the sudden death of Rev. Vatsaas, which, so soon after the murder of Gustaf Tornvall, further depleted the thin ranks of TEAM workers. At the time Christmas was being celebrated in Shanghai around tables that looked almost bare in comparison with the traditional feast in the homelands, thousands in Shensi were in the last agonies of starvation.

Christmas and the joy of reunion were also overshadowed by a serious eye infection which threatened Anna Englund's sight. Then, the family's prayers for her having been answered, she was again confined with the flu. Time again seemed to take an extra pair of wings and trunks and suitcases which had been excitedly unpacked were being reluctantly filled again for Miriam and Grace to return to the China Inland Mission school in Chefoo. While Anna, hardly recovered from her illness, rushed to get the girls ready for travel, her husband made fresh efforts to find help for countless sufferers in Shensi. The American Famine Relief Commission was unable to give much hope; the China Inland Mission was glad to share some relief funds; but as Englund once more began his journey he had only minimal funds compared to a need so gigantic that only God could remedy. Sharing the deepest feelings of his sympathetic heart, Englund wrote to the General Director, Rev. T. J. Bach, at the Mission headquarters in Chicago, "We almost dread to return to the field and face again all the suffering of the famine-stricken people."

The two-week school vacation came inevitably to its tear-stained end. The Englund family once more bound themselves together in prayer before facing another of the seemingly endless farewells, an inescapable part of a missionary career, at docks, rail and bus stations, and now airports. Other parents and children added to the confusion of laughter, tears, final promises and encouragements, and the flurry of trivialities which filled the terrible gap between the gangplank being pulled aboard and the ship lazily moving out to sea. Little Winifred looked up at her parents. "Grace and Miriam cried," she said solemnly, and William Englund and his wife, watching the tugs surrender the ship to the power of her own engines, reminded each other of that better land where there is no sea or parting or tears.

10

Courageous

The source of Englund's courage was an intimate communion with God through prayer and meditation on the Scriptures, and a warm fellowship with other Christians. With Rev. T. J. Bach he exchanged letters of mutual encouragement. "Be of good cheer Brother and Sister Englund. It is not the hard times that make character; they just reveal what is in the heart already," the General Director had written, and when the Englunds and three women missionaries boarded the train in Shanghai they knew that the hard times in Shensi were ahead of them.

The comfort of the first section of the journey was inevitably followed by opposite conditions on the second section. A car kindly sent from the Baptist Mission to meet them at the railhead was scarcely adequate for the six passengers and a truck for the baggage broke down 20 miles from home. Englund once more found himself spending a night on the kind of earthen bed that he had been introduced to 30 years earlier. The innkeeper's hurried attempts to get a fire going beneath the beds succeeded in warming only a fraction of the surface for part of the night. Except for their fur coats, the Englunds had only a single blanket to shelter them from the piercing winter cold, and Englund's sympathy spread even to their almost useless covering. "Never," he told his friends, "had those poor garments been pulled and stretched as they were that night." Dawn came with January tardiness and later in the day TEAM fellow missionaries arrived to take them to the city by car. Within an hour the great walls of Sian came into view.

Conditions were worse than reports to Shanghai indicated. Famine and drought had followed each other for six consecutive years. Another dry winter gave no hope of a summer harvest. Englund, with his pitifully small Famine Relief Fund, watched long lines of living skeletons stagger into the city like an army of dead men. Despair had driven them from their dusty, barren farms. Possessions and family had lost all value to them. Money alone mattered; it would buy a little food and delay the ultimate calamity of death. Life was unbearable, but death more to be feared, its terrible torments grimly portrayed in Buddhist temples. Men "without God and without hope" struggled to exist only because the alternative of death was even more dreadful. Markets were full of household goods and farm equipment made useless by harvest failures. Parents sold their children in a desperate effort to find money for food. As in a nightmare, Englund saw little girls being offered in the market for the equivalent of 50¢ (U.S.). As he watched he pleaded that God in wrath would remember mercy.

The widespread famine crushed all hope that new students would enroll in the Bible Institute, but the street chapel was open daily. The preachers would have gladly offered food as well as the gospel to their starving audiences but almost nothing was available either from secular or religious sources. North America, struggling with its own problem of depression, had little to spare for a remote province in far-off China. But the message preached offered a gift worth infinitely more than a bowl of noodles or a dish of steamed bread. The gracious offer of eternal life with an assured place in the Father's house far outvalued any generous offer of free meals, if that were possible, to prolong the misery of life on earth.

Englund plunged into his many duties, trying to catch up with work accumulated during his two months in Shanghai. In spite of extreme difficulty in following any discussion because of deafness, he had been urged to continue as a member of the China Field Council. The Central Committee of the new Chinese Association of Churches also needed his presence. Auditors were impatiently waiting for him to close the treasurer's books for the year while correspondence from Chicago headquarters also clamored for a reply. As soon as spring came, however, Englund squeezed in a visit to Lantien.

Abundant rain had broken the long drought and people were cheerfully splashing through puddles and bubbling streams. Cars and trucks sank deep in the mud so often that Englund decided a mule would be more reliable for this trip. The chosen animal balked, not sharing in the general rejoicing over a change of weather and spoiled by the luxury of city life, strongly resenting having to slosh over country roads. With neither spirit to face the challenge nor strength to tackle the mud, the mule earned a dishonorable discharge, and was replaced by a cow hired from a friendly farmer. God's ambassador was traveling third class! By evening the plodding beast had faithfully carried Englund and his fellow worker, Teacher Huang, as far as Yeh-hu. With only six more miles to Lantien, they anticipated no difficulty in arriving the following morning in time for the first service.

The cow evidently had other ideas of what constituted a Sabbath day's journey and adjusted her speed accordingly. People already gathered for morning worship sighed with relief when they saw the animal leisurely amble into the church yard, and they whispered excitedly that the pastors had arrived at last for the conference.

It was amazing that anyone had arrived. For most people, a good meal was only a memory. Transportation from villages to the city either did not exist or was too expensive. Added physical exhaustion made distances along the muddy roads seem twice as far as usual and the constant danger of bandits contributed still more to the unpleasantness of travel. The offer of a ride to church in a 320 h.p. heated car, with a gospel program coming over its radio, or the sight of a Sunday school bus sent out to transport conference delegates would easily have convinced many Shensi Christians that the Millenium had dawned; especially if they were welcomed with unlimited supplies of hot coffee, donuts, pie and cookies ... but those country Christians were not looking at problems, they were looking for Christ. With clothes having patches on patches, their faces gaunt with hunger, they converged on Lantien. Women with bound feet encouraged each other. What their weak bodies lacked, God miraculously supplied. One elderly woman, her minute feet aching and her strength all gone, pleaded with the Lord to get her to church. "And, Lord," she concluded, "if I don't make it, then You will be the One who loses face, and not I!" Of course, she was there.

People did not come in vain. The Lord Himself met with them. Songs of joy and sounds of praise filled the church. Mr. Huang and William Englund both preached twice a day. Seventh Day Adventists had recently come into the district, and were unsettling some of the country churches by teaching the necessity of good works and observance of certain Old Testament laws for salvation. Englund dealt with the errors by teaching the Galatian epistle. By the time the conference ended much more had been accomplished than the correction of wrong doctrine. Men and women were so convicted of sin by the Holy Spirit that they broke into tears and made open confession. Many accepted Christ as Savior and with exhuberant rejoicing 13 believers were baptized.

A conference at Hsingping followed, with Englund speaking twice a day. The church building, extended to seat over 1,000 people, was too small for the crowds, and at least 200 had to stand by the open windows. Sinners were overwhelmed by an awful sense of God's presence. One man sprang to his feet, and the audience in horrified silence heard the sobbing confession that he had committed murder. Christians also made public confession and sought forgiveness from God and man. In a happy letter to friends Englund wrote, "There was an atmosphere of prayer which truly gave air under the wings of the messages from the Word. The pastor rejoiced greatly and said it was the best conference they had known for years. Glory be to God. His work is going on from victory to victory." But as Englund bowed farewell to Pastor Kuo and others of the Hsingping church, a cool wind sprang up like a sinister reminder that no harvest is safe from disaster. It brought a May night frost whitening the fields and blasting hopes for an early crop of grain.

Cruel winds of another kind were blowing. Soon after Englund's return to Sian, Mr. Eliassen and a Chinese assistant of the International Famine Relief were held for ransom by bandits a few miles north of the city. After 19 days of rumors, uncertainty and danger, the men were rescued unharmed by provincial troops. Englund meanwhile, due to the dangers of travel, was refused permission to visit Kienhsien where the church was looking forward to having him as speaker for their spring conference.

In midsummer the Chinese Association of Churches arranged a ten day conference in which Englund was asked to have a giant share by teaching the complete book of Daniel in 17 sessions. Dr. Zwemer, world famous as a missionary to Moslems, unexpectedly arrived and was invited to speak at the opening session. Sian, with a Mohammedan population of 30,000, had attracted his attention. A shade temperature of 100° outside the building exactly equalled the number of delegates inside the building, but summer heat did not divert attention from God's Word, and the final session was a service of consecration in which prayer, praise and tears were mingled. When the entire company stood together, hands raised to Heaven as they sang Pastor Hsi's hymn, "I will offer up my whole heart, I will offer up my whole body," William Englund felt God's Spirit sway the gathering as if the mighty wind of Pentecost were blowing again.

The same wind stirred again when the Bible Institute opened at the end of August, 1933. With more than 20 new students enrolled, classes had hardly begun when David Chou, an evangelist from Shanghai, arrived. His dialect was difficult for Shensi ears, but his earnestness and fervency in preaching and praying overcame the problem of communication. What had happened earlier in the year in Lantien, Hsingping and at the Sian church leaders' conference was repeated in the Bible school. Young men fell on their faces in God's fiery presence, confessing sin and giving themselves afresh to Him.

David Chou's ministry was followed by a visit from two energetic workers of the newly formed Bethel Evangelistic Band, also from Shanghai. Heavy rain prevented their keeping an appointment in Kienhsien, but arrangements were quickly made for special services in the Bible school chapel, which became so crowded that a move was made to a large church west of the city. The Spirit of God moved mightily, arousing hundreds of people to realize their urgent need of a Savior. So great was the response that the Bethel Band was invited to visit every place in Shensi and Kansu where TEAM workers were stationed. The coming of these Spirit-filled, earnest Chinese evangelists, Englund declared to be one of the greatest encouragements he had seen since entering China.

When TEAM missionaries met in Pingliang for the 1933 conference there were more reasons than usual for thanksgiving, not the least being that they had all arrived safely. Anna Englund was sufficiently recovering from sickness to be able to leave the hospital and travel with her husband. After a two day delay due to torrential rain, the Englunds, Ahlstrands and Gustafsons advanced from the city, ready to do battle with mud and swollen rivers. Their brave little convoy was the Mission bus and a private car, but horsepower was not enough. Men, mules and an occasional cow were needed to drag the vehicles through the worst sections. Flood water stalled the engines and marooned passengers were carried ashore on the backs of Chinese farmers. Travel became "digging, skidding, climbing, walking, pulling, pushing and plowing through mud and rain," wrote Englund. The bus and car seemed almost a handicap. After five days the muddy party arrived in Pingliang, thankful to God that there had been neither accident nor breakdown, and that Red bandits, reported to be in ambush near the main road, had not attacked them.

The conference was the best for years. Revival, which earlier had been transforming Chinese churches, now renewed the missionaries. With rain falling continuously for a full week after the conference business ended, TEAM workers were shut in with God, each day bringing an ever deeper sense of His holy presence and power.

The bad weather had not improved what was optimistically called the main road to Sian, but the returning party was more experienced in techniques for dealing with deep mud and swollen rivers. As they sloshed and slithered home, Englund spent part of the time translating a Swedish chorus into English. With a broad smile he shared his poetic effort with his travel companions:

> Onward it goes, O yes, onward it goes,
> Jesus our Captain fully everything knows;
> Victory have we in the Lord's blessed name,
> Though strong foes surround us,
> We go on the same.

They all sang the song triumphantly as they lugged the car out of the last mud hole. Ahead was the city of Sian. Ahead was sure victory in the supreme name of Jesus Christ. God was marching majestically among His people. It had been a wonderful year of advance. Like Paul on the highway to Rome, they thanked God and took courage.

William and Anna Englund were glad to be back in the Bible school where Mrs. Vatsaas had competently filled in for the three weeks of their absence. They also eagerly anticipated having their two daughters home from school for the Christmas vacation. It would be the first time in six years that the girls had been in Sian.

11

A Man of Prayer

To title any particular chapter in the story of William Englund "A man of prayer" is very misleading. His whole life was saturated with prayer. Every day was a fresh experience of meeting with God. Few people knew exactly at what hour he arose to pour out his heart in praise and intercession. His children remember that no matter how early they got up their father was already shut in his room praying aloud, and his wife Anna, who knew him best, testifies that between 4:30 and 5:00 o'clock, summer and winter, William Englund was preparing to seek audience with his King. Normally once a week, and on special occasions, he would eat neither breakfast nor noon meal but continue resolutely in what he called "fighting the Devil." He learned that prayer is not struggling with a reluctant God, but wrestling with a resistant enemy. The battle often exhausted him. In private, he prayed in Swedish, using his own list of people and churches for which he had a special concern. He also faithfully remembered his fellow missionaries, systematically going over their names printed in the Mission Prayer Calendar. Then at 7:30 breakfast time he was ready to lead his family and any guests in Bible reading and prayer.

There was nothing about which William Englund did not pray. He took literally the invitation to "be careful for nothing; but in every thing by prayer and supplication with thanksgiving let your requests be made known unto God." Everything was confidently brought to God's attention—TB of the lungs, language study, bedbugs, rain, revival, sickness, finance, guidance, his family, a mule struggling in a flooded river, the Bible school, churches in China and other lands. The list had no end. Rev. Roy Brehm, writing for the General Director, had once reminded his "dear fellow worker" that the apostolic method of solving problems and carrying on the work was, "BUT we will give ourselves CONTINUALLY to PRAYER and to the ministry of the WORD." And 1934 proved to be a year in which Englund needed to exercise the privilege of prayer to the full. One crisis was intensely personal. Others were alarmingly large.

Englund's hearing had become progressively worse. He had given up the cumbersome old ear trumpet which collected sound without amplifying it. Esther Staalesen had brought to China a wonderful new Acousticon marketed by the Dictograph Products Company. Grandfather of modern hearing aids and enormous in comparison, it operated on batteries which were not easily found in the troubled Northwest. Englund was thankful for it, and glad to pass on the ear trumpet to a Lantien elder also going deaf. When Englund aimed his powerful voice at the trumpet and the elder shouted at the Acousticon, both of them had a noisy time of fellowship. But such happy interludes could not hold back the incoming tide of total silence which was to cut off William Englund from the sound of voices he loved most and the affectionate greetings of a multitude of friends. Some of his fellow missionaries met specifically to pray that God would miraculously heal and Englund himself earnestly pleaded that he would not totally lose his hearing, especially as it seemed so necessary in his ministry. He struggled over the question of why God was allowing such a handicap to occur. How could a deaf man counsel Bible school students, or effectively help unbelievers seeking Christ? Or take an intelligent part in committee meetings? Or know how others were being led to pray in a prayer meeting? Was his future to be marooned on a lonely island in a sea of silence?

One night Englund shared the problem with God and by morning the answer came. "Some vessels have ears; others are without ears," was the word to his listening heart. Familiar with Chinese kitchen pots and tableware, he understood. With or without handles, all had a purpose. Englund had never doubted God's ability to heal, but now he submitted without complaint to God's wisdom. He never became suspicious that people were taking advantage of his deafness to talk about him and he never lost his sense of humor. While continuing to use his battery powered hearing aid, he would sometimes say to long-winded friends, "It costs me money to listen to you!"

William and Anna were again separated from their children when the two girls returned to school soon after the New Year. A small consolation was that improved transportation had brought school and home closer together in travel time. Little Jack Bell even traveled by plane from Sian to his home in Lanchow, taking only six hours, instead of the usual 36 days and, as Englund constantly reminded his family, contact via the throne of grace would never be broken. His prayers were ever for his children and they liked to share their problems with him because, as one of them said, "We feel God had an open ear to father."

If ever there was a time when men needed to pray it was 1934, the year when everything happened. China was still using the old calendar and New Year celebrations came long after the Western world had impatiently rushed into another year. Two evangelists of the Bethel Band arrived and Englund with Bible school teachers, students and fellow missionaries enthusiastically joined a campaign to reach Sian for Christ. Multitudes enjoying the vacation had opportunities all day long to hear the gospel. Morning services were at the Y.M.C.A., afternoon gatherings were in a large tent at the Bible Institute and evening sessions in a new chapel next to the Mission home. By the time the campaign ended more than 300 men and women had accepted Christ.

Prayer was also answered for the development of Chinese churches. The March conference of representatives under the outstanding leadership of Pastor Kuo Ming-yueh gave abundant evidence of increasing ability and rich spiritual gifts. Alert delegates, with keen insight into basic issues, spent most of the five days considering spiritual matters, and were all encouraged by a report from the first Chinese home missionary on his work in Kansu province. Other matters were not forgotten and William Englund was elected treasurer for another two years. The conference was a prelude to such a mighty demonstration of God's power in Shensi province that one missionary wrote, "Souls are falling before the convicting power of the Spirit like grain before the sickle."

A timely letter from the home office reminded Englund that "in those days when the number of disciples was multiplied, there arose a murmuring." The murmuring began in the kitchen of the Bible Institute. For the enemy, knowing the strategic importance of the school, struck there first. It was a trifling affair, but, as Englund said, "the Devil is an expert in making an elephant out of a mouse if he can stir up trouble and hinder the Lord's work." A day of prayer and fasting was the remedy, but before classes could be resumed a number of rebellious students were expelled. When some pleaded for readmission they were required to show practical evidence of repentance and to obtain a fresh recommendation from their home churches.

The battle was resumed when about 200 church workers met for their summer Bible conference. The theme for the nine days was "Victory," and Englund warned that since the Devil is very allergic to such a subject, special opposition might occur. He quoted, "When the sons of God came to present themselves before the Lord, Satan came also," and added that the Devil is not afraid to attend a Bible conference. In fact, the enemy's agent was in the congregation. At the end of the first service, he strode towards Englund and tried to force him from the platform, screaming, "Let all those who are the running dogs of the foreigners leave the church." Christians responded by singing so loudly that the intruder's voice was smothered. Ignorant of God's promise to Englund that "no weapon that is formed against thee shall prosper," the same man tried to attack during the afternoon session but was quickly evicted by an elder.

The devastating heat was not so easily dealt with. The thermometer rose higher each day of the conference until it reached a scorching 118 degrees. People were dying in the blistering streets and for Englund to preach twice a day was not easy, but let him tell the secret of his strength in those searing days. "The prayer of many truehearted intercessors was answered with daily strength for the Lord's needy servant. We felt His presence. There was a solemn hush and soul-refreshing atmosphere at the meetings. The Spirit moved hearts. Prayer and praise flowed like a mighty river towards the throne of God from souls unitedly poured out before Him. In the cool of the evening, when the shadows of night gradually enveloped all, it was a beautiful and inspiring sight to see the white-clad crowd sitting in a semicircle in front of the tent, singing stirring hymns, uniting in prayer, or following each other with joyful testimonies."

As Englund and his fellow missionaries waged war against the power of darkness in the name of the Lord Most High, they simultaneously struggled with acute financial problems. The value of the U.S. dollar had fallen and funds were so short that, by the middle of February, no remittance had been received for the previous quarter. A missionary family with three children in school was alarmed to find that tuition and boarding expenses swallowed up their total income for six months. An exchange of letters between the Mission office in Chicago and the Port-O-Phone Corporation tells the story from another angle.

Englund's hearing aid had been sent home for repairs. The company wrote that the cost would be $3.89, and suggested trading in the old machine for a greatly improved one for a balance payment of $32.50. The Mission's reply included the cryptic sentence, "We regret the inability of purchasing the later model as described in your letter." It was even more impossible to find a modest $500 to repair the ceilings, walls and roof of the crumbling Memorial School building in Sian . . . and Englund had difficulty in explaining to his Chinese brethren that only $100 had been received from rich America to assist the work of six Chinese churches for another three months. Prayer was again the only recourse.

Deafness and tight finances did not deter Englund from evangelism. He was able to join the Bethel Band in concluding their Shensi tour with a campaign in Lantien. He had with him little Tulick Vatsaas and his own daughter Winifred, then three and a half years old. Not only were the children a great attraction, but Winifred was asked to sing a selection of Chinese choruses. Encouraged by the response, she repeated her full repertoire to curious soldiers and townsmen gathered at the door of the house where the Englunds were staying. Since there was no evangelist at hand, she concluded by saying, "And now you must all believe in Jesus."

Lantien was again being troubled by Seventh Day Adventists, who had forced themselves upon the church with abuse and threats, occupying part of the premises and preparing to take over the whole work. By prayer alone, Englund and others removed the intruders. The hearts of the congregation were also prepared by intercession for further teaching from God's Word and sinners daily turned to Christ.

Night time, however, had its difficulties. The room where Englund and Swenson (his companion) slept was so small that two camp beds almost filled it. The ceiling of bamboo mats served as a community center for rats and mice. Tired after a long, happy day, Englund tried to ignore a strange crawling sensation around his legs, but the disturbance was too persistent to be ignored. In desperation he called to Swenson who grabbed a stick while Englund directed operations with a flashlight. "Convincing evidence soon came to view showing that some animal must have shared my bed for quite a time," wrote Englund afterwards. Excitement rose as the bed covers were slowly rolled back. Swenson, quivering with excitement, held the stick ready for the kill. Englund breathlessly sought out the enemy with his flashlight beam. Swenson struck like lightning, but the mouse was even quicker. And the silence of the night was shattered by a burst of laughter from the two men. They tried a more successful tactic, occasionally switching on the flashlight to keep the errant mouse in its proper place in the ceiling, but an enormous rat with a tail as thick as rope crept with sinister silence into the little room and drove all sleep out.

Boyhood memories of winter in Minnesota were revived as Englund and his companion started back to Sian. A fierce snowstorm and bitter winds made it difficult for them to keep their eyes open. In one deep gully, part of a precipitous hillside had crashed down, blocking their passage. While Englund stood alone in the mud and snow crying to God to prevent more of the hill from burying him and the mulecart, Swenson and the muleteer ran through the blinding storm to borrow a pickax and a shovel from a temple. With the road finally cleared they struggled on, wet and tired, to the next market town.

The only shelter was a small space under the shafts of the cart where they set up their camp cots and spread out their soaking bedding. A charcoal fire was their sole hope of drying clothes but proved insignificant against the bitter cold. The following morning even the mule could not force its way through the deep drifts. Their one choice was to leave the buried road and make for the open fields. The two missionaries hitched themselves to the cart and triumphantly hauled it and the mule up a steep bank to higher ground, while the gloomy muleteer watched the operation in silence. When success came, he smiled and held up both thumbs as a tribute to missionary manpower. Even with this herculean effort they covered only two miles in half a day.

Swenson volunteered to struggle ahead to Sian and bring back help. Englund waited in the home of the muleteer's friend where he had the special privilege of being the first to preach Christ in that village. Late the following afternoon a rescue party arrived and the next morning they all started out for Sian. The animals could do no more than carry baggage and as Englund plodded through the deep snow he soon lost the heel of one shoe. He hobbled home at noon. It was Thanksgiving Day, 1934. He was exhausted but satisfied and glad to be in the Lord's service. He summarized the experience by quoting T. J. Bach: "It is always first class where God is." The muleteer and his animal may not have had such an enlightened view.

News in Sian again called for urgent prayer. From the Coast came an alarming report that a Chinese ship, carrying many missionary children back to school in Chefoo, had been captured by pirates. The Englunds knew that their children were not aboard but shared in the concern of other parents. Prayer was answered. None of the children suffered harm and ever after lived in the glow of an adventure which put them head and shoulders above all those who had not had the good fortune even to see a pirate.

The situation in Sian was even more disturbing. Communist troops, 6,000 strong, had occupied a mountain district south of the city and approached to within 30 miles of Lantien. All missionaries were once more called within the massive shelter of Sian's walls, while the military governor led a slow campaign against the enemy. Three months later the missionaries were still pinned down in the city. One afternoon as a group of TEAM missionaries were talking of God's mighty power in contrast to man's feeble efforts, they were startled by Mr. C. Carwardine, of the China Inland Mission, bursting in with news that he and others had barely escaped with their lives when communist forces had overrun the southern part of the province. Then he broke down, saying that Mr. and Mrs. S. C. Frencham had been captured and killed. Telegrams began to pour in, followed by letters describing incredible suffering as missionary families struggled through snow and ice on mountain trails. Without extra clothes or bedding, some parents had carried small children for ten days. Mr. Carwardine trudged back through the cruel mountains in the hope of finding survivors. Soldiers escaping from advancing communists told him that they had seen Mr. Frencham's head on a pole outside a city gate.

As Carwardine continued his lonely patrol, missionaries in Sian continued in prayer. Six weeks later they received a telegram with news that the Frenchams were alive and well in Hanchung. Like the Jerusalem disciples who could not believe that God had delivered Peter from prison in answer to prayer, the Sian missionaries decided the report was too marvelous to be true. Then a second message confirmed the first and released a burst of praise. Englund, thinking of Daniel's preservation from hungry lions, heartily rejoiced that God is still "the living God, stedfast for ever . . . He delivers and rescues, and He works signs and wonders in heaven and in earth." Never have God's people prayed in vain.

A different kind of problem suddenly mushroomed. Sian authorities ordered all buildings along the main road to be pulled down within 20 days as part of a street widening plan. Englund wrestled with the difficulty of having to cut off 20 feet from the chapel building and to move all other buildings connected with it in the time allotted, with neither funds in hand nor help from the city. Once more his eyes turned to the Lord who had foreseen the need and who would provide. In a simple understatement to T. J. Bach, he wrote, "We are kept very busy." His responsibilities were carefully considered at the spring, 1935, conference. At that time he continued as the treasurer for all Shensi missionaries; he was one of the two overseers of the new Chinese church organization and a frequent speaker at conferences; bore responsibility for repairs and alterations to his own mission buildings in Sian and, above all else, spent a great part of his time in prayer. The conference questioned whether it was reasonable to ask him to continue as principal of the Bible school, since he felt this required his enthusiastic participation in evangelism with the students. No substitute could be found among the few remaining missionaries, but, in faith, a decision was made to continue the school. Englund's load was lightened by inviting the former head teacher, Mr. Hsieh, to help in the class work. It was also expected that street widening and the altering of the chapel would temporarily interrupt nightly services by the Bible school staff and students, and give Englund a chance to catch his breath.

They underestimated his eagerness to make Christ known. He decided on an intensive drive in the west suburb of the city as an alternate opportunity, and, except when heavy rain fell, services were held in front of the Bible school every afternoon. Teachers and students were involved in 14 evangelistic services a week, spurred on by their indefatigable leader, William Englund. It was not in vain. On the busy street men and women urgently called on God, not ashamed to pray openly for salvation.

Anna Englund was busy, too. Her special responsibility, apart from being ears for her deaf husband, was a fast developing work among women. On Wednesdays she visited the provincial jail with a Chinese companion and every week traveled to three country churches for women's meetings. Other well-trained Bible women took the gospel to villages all around Sian, and energetically followed up tent campaigns in the country. Neatly dressed, smiling and carrying a large Bible, the women hobbled on their tiny bound feet from house to house, and soon were accepted as a welcome part of village life. Many new believers were strengthened in the faith and taught in the Scriptures while numerous others were brought to Christ. God was building His church in city, town and village. God's Spirit was giving generous gifts to His Chinese people. An abundant harvest was being reaped in answer to prayer and in spite of troubled times.

Now William Englund suffered the waning of his physical strength. Harsh winters, constant travel, continual preaching and teaching, all during a time of war, banditry and financial difficulties, had drained his vitality. A checkup at the Sian hospital showed one lung to be affected. His responsibilities at the Bible school were taken over by Mr. R. W. Middleton, a China Inland Mission worker temporarily driven out of his own area by communist forces. Anna courageously took over the remainder of her husband's heavy load. In the midst of the crisis, a well-known evangelist, Rev. Leland Wang, arrived for two days of special services and stayed with the Englunds.

Chinese Christians had flocked to the city and on the second evening a large group met in front of the Bible school to pray. As people prayed outside the house, Leland Wang and Mrs. Englund prayed inside, anointing William Englund in the name of the Lord. God answered so marvelously that when he arrived in Chefoo doctors could find no trace of the trouble. Nevertheless, rest was needed to regain his strength and progress was accelerated by the joy of again being united with the Englund daughters, resident students in Chefoo at the time.

As Englund enjoyed warm summer weather and cool breezes from the Pacific he looked back over the previous year and a half with great praise to God. Chinese churches had worked more closely with each other than ever before and forged close bonds with their missionary brethren. There had been miraculous protection in times of danger. He had seen God meet every kind of need when all human resources failed. Supernatural energy had been given him for a supernatural task. Then, just before leaving for the Coast, he had joyfully witnessed the graduation of sixteen students from the Bible school. God had called His Elijah to a time of temporary rest, but there were 16 Elishas to carry on the work with the same flaming passion and boundless enthusiasm as their loved and respected teacher. Prayer had been answered over and over again. "We praised God for His goodness in every way," Englund wrote from the quiet of Chefoo.

12

Evangelist

The Scriptures make a distinction between evangelists and teachers, but in Englund the gifts were combined. When he taught the Scriptures, Christians were encouraged, strengthened and often convicted of tolerated sins; at the same time unbelievers were converted. God's Word was a mightily effective weapon in the hand of William Gideon Englund. His heart, therefore, was full of praise to God when Dr. Handley Stockley at the Sian English Baptist hospital held up both thumbs to indicate that his smiling patient had passed all tests and was ready again for action.

The Bible Institute had accepted 20 students for three months of basic studies, which included the Gospel of John, the Acts, the Epistle to the Romans, a short outline of church history and instruction in music. Study was translated into action every evening when students and staff preached in the crowded street chapel. The less gifted or more timid were assigned the strategic task of encouraging passers-by to "please enter and listen a while to the good sounding news." The fervent spirit of Englund and his Chinese staff was so contagious that before long every student was eager for an opportunity to witness. Saturday was a big day. The whole school fanned out over the countryside, preaching in dozens of villages and seeing scores of people turn to Christ.

From far away Denver came other encouragement. Opening the mail, Englund found a gift of $60 towards the support of a Chinese Bible school teacher. Training men and women for effective service was the cornerstone of Mission strategy and staffing the school with qualified Chinese teachers was an essential part of that policy. Finance was a critical item. As Englund credited the $60 to the Bible school

83

account, he paused to thank God for another answered prayer.

TEAM missionaries in Sian were excited. For over a year Englund had been exchanging long letters with the General Director, Rev. T. J. Bach, in preparation for his visit to China. No travel agency existed to arrange an itinerary from Chicago through Japan to Mongolia, including stops in Chefoo, Tientsin, Peking, Kalgan and Sian; and a precise hour-by-hour schedule for visitors to China was an impossibility. Responsibility fell on the veteran traveler, William Englund, whose long experience with irregular trains, stubborn mules, pioneer buses and cars, swollen rivers, muddy roads, bedbugs and bombings, fully qualified him. But even an expert could not plan the unexpected.

Mr. Bach had emphasized that he did not want any publicity since he was coming "just as a servant of the Lord's servants," and looked forward not only to seeing large mature churches, but also pioneer country efforts and areas where the gospel had not yet reached. The point about publicity was well understood, but nothing could restrain Chinese Christians from planning a big reception at the Sian railroad station. TEAM missionaries were also preparing a rousing welcome for their General Director. On the evening before the great day, T. J. Bach walked into Sian Mission headquarters unmet and unannounced. A letter announcing his change of schedule had not arrived and Mr. Bach had found himself relying on God alone as he struggled with baggage, coolies, rickshaw men, an unknown language, and the happy confusion of the Sian terminal.

The General Director's visit coincided with a great surge of blessing in Northwest China. At Hsingping it was as if the very wind of Heaven swept over a congregation of more than 1,000 people . . . and in six days of special Bible teaching in Sian, Christians were renewed, sinners converted, 31 people baptized and financial giving was unusually generous.

At regular services in the church "the Lord added to them day by day those that were being saved." Soldiers responded in great numbers. Officers in charge of 300 men billeted near to the Mission visited Englund to invite him to preach to the troops immediately. He was, of course, delighted to respond, and as a result most of the men began to attend a special daily service in the church. Within a short time 40 of the soldiers had accepted Christ. Visits to the provincial women's jail by Anna Englund and her Chinese co-workers had increased to six a week and had considerable influence. When Englund and three other missionaries called on the superintendent of the men's prison, they were asked to hold an evangelistic service right away and to return regularly. In both jails men and women eagerly turned to Christ for pardon.

In that same year of blessing, the church in Huhsien enjoyed a wonderful five-day conference. At times the whole congregation seemed melted in prayer before God and every evening Englund rejoiced to see people being counseled after the service. Heavy rain, mud, and soldiers on the church premises kept him and Mr. Bach from visiting Lantien, but they were able to reach Kienhsien where the church had experienced a stormy beginning 40 years earlier. A landlord who had rented premises to the first missionary was thrown into jail for the crime and the house demolished. A year later Adolf Gustafson made a new attempt to enter the city but was struck down with sickness within a few months. As he lay dying, he cried out, "Hallelujah, we've won!" His words were prophetic. When T. J. Bach stood to preach in the historic church, with Julius Bergstrom as interpreter, 1,000 people were waiting to hear the Word of God, and by the time the conference ended, others had been brought to Christ.

On the way home from similar times of blessing in Chin-tu, Englund noticed an earth mound about 30 feet high. Climbing to the top with Teacher Hsieh, they found a stone tablet in honor of the inventor of writing. According to the inscription, the originator of Chinese characters had been inspired by the footsteps of birds on the mound, said to be about 5,000 years old. Englund turned to Mr. Hsieh. "I am very thankful that God has so marvelously used the Chinese invention of printing to spread the gospel," he said, "but I sometimes wish that the inventor of your intricate characters had hit on some simpler form of writing."

The year 1935 had another interesting flashback. An alert historian noted that it was the 1300th anniversary of Nestorians coming to Sian. Chinese Christians and the missionary community met for a celebration at the "Grove of Stone Tablets," belonging to the Sian Museum. The famous "Nestorian stone" had a place of honor in a small building by itself. It records a missionary movement which originated with the Council of Ephesus in 432 A.D. There Nestorius, bishop of Constantinople, was condemned for his belief that Christ had a dual personality, one human and one divine, within a living consciousness. In spite of condemnation, the erring bishop carried most of the Syrian churches with him, and inspired his followers with a missionary zeal which impelled them into central Asia, and finally to China. As Bishop Shen of the Church Mission reviewed Nestorian history at the anniversary service, he pointed out that compromise with Chinese tradition and religions left only a stone and a few ruins to mark their efforts.

Years earlier, Fredrik Franson, founder of The Evangelical Alliance Mission, had seen the same stone and noticed a dragon carved at the top and a turtle at the bottom. He remarked on the significance of mythical creatures being at the head and base of a Christian monument which fails to make clear reference to the cross of Jesus Christ. The turtle represented a fabulous animal, said to have existed in the time of the great Wu, founder of the first Chinese dynasty in 2205 B.C. With supernatural strength it dug a tunnel through a mountain so that a river could flow on a different course. Toleration of ancient superstitions had neutralized the efforts of the Nestorians and converts had reverted to their former way of living. Dragon and turtle had never been dethroned.

Threatening moves by Japan compelled the North Eastern University in Peking to relocate in Sian. It was part of a great trek of "down-river people" who left their ancestral homes in East China to find sanctuary in the West. Englund saw it as a new opportunity for evangelism and opened the Bible school for a Sunday afternoon English Bible class to be taught by Mr. Swenson. As he explained in a letter home, "What we mainly seem to lack is time for getting everything done."

The long economic depression in the homelands continued to create great financial problems for missionaries. An exchange rate which fluctuated in China's favor added to their difficulties. As Field Treasurer, Englund was daily faced with the reality of inadequate funds. Compared to our modern cost of living the needs of those days seem extremely modest. The yearly support for a missionary was $500 (U.S.). An allowance of $100 a year was made for children of school age and half that for those younger. Englund figured quickly with his pencil: 28 missionaries, 11 children in school, four under school age; add travel costs, and the total need for the year was $15,600. Evangelism, educational and general expenses for 20 churches and two Bible schools required another $6,000. Thinking of old mission homes falling apart, he hopefully included an item of $220 for repairs, giving a total budget of $21,800. The amount looked enormous and before continuing work on the accounts Englund thankfully remembered that God will "supply all your need according to His riches in glory by Christ Jesus." There was other encouragement. Ten Chinese women who had been financially supported during childhood by the Mission joined together to pay the salary of a local Bible woman and to pray regularly for her. The Chinese church in the Northwest was indeed maturing.

Chinese cities were not the quietest of places. Days and nights were punctuated by the rattle of mah-jong pieces interspersed with occasional loud quarrels; by the squeal of pigs reluctant to fulfill their destiny of providing ham for a feast; by temple gongs and throbbing drums; or by the sharp crack of a rifle, fired to frighten robbers or arouse sky dragons to fight so that storms and rain might come. Liberal use of bicycle bells and car horns, together with warning shouts from sturdy rickshaw coolies and cheerful calls from vendors of hot food and sweetmeats, added to the hubbub of the old cities.

All sounds were extremely dim to Englund. His battery powered hearing aid no longer gave much help. It was, he wrote, "getting old and poor like its owner," and he pleaded for a more powerful model, "their strongest one, with amplifiers and bone conduction devices at-

tached. Whatever the kind, I must have the loudest on the market."
A new Acousticon was sent, but proved a disappointment. The "bone
conduction device," designed to by-pass the deteriorated nerves of
the ear, was not a success. Englund felt vibrations, but heard no sound.
With his usual good humor, he speculated that his head was too
dense to respond to the device!

He wrote an urgent letter asking for a double transmitter and
stronger battery. The equipment was shipped immediately with the
advice that batteries be kept in an upright position. Friends at home
paid for the new Acousticon, including the Chinese customs duty.
Englund himself appeared at the office "as living proof of his own
deaf self, which all went to show that the apparatus was no luxury
device but a most important necessity." The officials generously
classified the hearing device as a medical instrument, reducing the
duty from 40 per cent to 10 per cent. But a better hearing aid, generosity of friends, and considerate customs officers could not hold
off much longer the day when William Englund would be shut into
a totally silent world. His wife, whom he sometimes called the "Queen
of Englund," was to become his ears.

As if sensing the urgency of those days, Englund refused to be halted by difficulty or danger. Irregular movements of communist forces
created general uneasiness in the province, but the Bible Institute accepted a class of 12 new students for a two-year course. Englund also
accepted responsibility for the annual Bible conference of Christian
workers scheduled to meet in Wukung. The summer of 1936 was exceptionally hot and humid. With Elder Chiang he learned at the bus
station that bus service had been canceled because of heavy rain.
Hurrying to the railroad station, they boarded a train which took them
to the halfway point of Hsingping. Rain had ceased and the hot sun
was combining extreme heat with the moist air. Two hours of waiting
was rewarded with a rumor that the "connecting" train would arrive
in late evening. Englund appreciated an invitation from the local
Chinese pastor to rest in the church. Christians quickly prepared a
couch by pushing several benches together and provided a brick for
a pillow.

Englund had settled comfortably for his afternoon siesta when a
deacon rushed in to announce the arrival of the express. He and Elder
Chiang hurried back to the station to find something different from
what they had expected.

A freight train, made up of flat cars loaded with iron rails and road-
making materials, was waiting for passengers. They joined the crowd
climbing aboard. The effect of sitting on scorching rails was similar to
that of having a Turkish bath. Englund noted the long rows of patient Chinese, their faces lined with streams of perspiration, and
afterwards wrote that he had traveled by "steamliner."

As the hot afternoon wore on, an earthquake rocked the area but made no impression on the passengers who were already being shaken to pieces by the rough track. The freight train jolted to a stop five miles short of its destination. A broken bridge was the cause. Englund and his companion walked to the city, hot, thirsty and tired. In the following eight days he taught the entire Epistle of I Corinthians to the 200 conference delegates. "The heat was melting but the spiritual atmosphere even more so," he reported.

After his visit to China, T. J. Bach summarized the problems as being *three Rs*: Reds, Robbers and Ruts. The first R brought the year 1936 to a dramatic close, and prompted a cable from Jersey City arriving at the headquarters of The Evangelical Alliance Mission, reading, "PLEASE WIRE BY WESTERN UNION COLLECT ANY INFORMATION REGARDING SAFETY OF REVEREND ENGLUND SIAN CHINA."

On December 14, Englund and his wife were startled from sleep by the chatter of machine guns and the crack of rifles. Sian was filled with confusion and wild rumors. Eventually the incredible truth filtered through. Generalissimo Chiang Kai-shek had been taken prisoner by one of his own army commanders and his personal bodyguards killed to the last man. The Generalissimo had gone to Sian to order Marshal Chang Hsueh-liang to launch a vigorous offensive against the last communist stronghold. The Marshal's preference was to unite with the Chinese communists against the common enemy, Japan.

Forces loyal to Chiang Kai-shek surrounded Sian, once more trapping missionaries within the high walls. Marshal Chang's troops, although ready to cooperate with communists, showed no hostility to Christians or foreigners. They were, in fact, happy to have nearly 100 people of various nationalities inside the city as an insurance against a bombing attack. Thirty planes circling overhead demonstrated that the danger was real. Civil war seemed imminent. The history of Northwest China was again being written in blood.

Tension and uncertainty continued for two long weeks. In the vortex of China's internal strife, Englund took advantage of being confined to Sian by catching up on Mission business. When an opportunity came for smuggling out a letter, with the help of a friendly pilot, he apologized to the General Director for his long delay in writing, and added that he was experiencing afresh that "God is our refuge and strength, a very present help in times of trouble."

Christmas Day dawned. Celebrations were impossible, but peace of heart was a fresh gift from above. Within the city, feverish defense preparations were being made. Outside the walls, government forces readied for battle. Christians spent long hours in prayer. The Generalissimo and his captor negotiated in critical arguments which would determine China's future. Then a miracle happened, Chiang Kai-shek was released and flew to Nanking with Marshal Chang. Everyone immediately assumed that all problems had been solved and conditions would improve.

The opposite was true. Large numbers of communist soldiers from Kansu province swarmed into Shensi to join Sian revolutionaries. Strong government armies tensed for an attack. Wide trenches were dug around the entire city and bomb shelters prepared. Englund decided to close the Bible Institute. "It all came so unexpectedly," he wrote, "but the Lord's assurance again proved a strength and comfort. Our gracious Master spoke in the midst of the storm, waves and darkness. The final meeting was touching. With tears and sobs, our united prayers ascended to the Throne of Grace, as, surrounded by danger and uncertainty, we commended each other to our Father's loving care."

The Chinese government and foreign embassies were equally anxious to evacuate all non-Chinese from Sian, but military authorities in the city were reluctant to let their hostages go. Foreigners had become pawns in the deadly game of war. Few telegrams reached the city and mail was often destroyed. Representatives of the British and American Embassies flew into the city for two weeks of fruitless discussions. Englund, expecting better results through prayer, was not disappointed.

The Chinese manager of the best hotel in town joined the missionaries in their prayer meeting and the following day invited them all to lunch. Captain Scott, the British representative staying in the same hotel, again contacted the military authorities and came back with the good news that travel permits would be issued the following day. God's planning and provision were perfect as usual. Karl Hill, of missionary parents, had an automobile agency in Sian and provided three trucks for the journey to Shanghai.

The next morning, after a traditional two-hour delay for an unnecessary check on travel documents, the party of 77 people departed. After 50 miles they came to no man's land. Karl Hill, experienced in China travel, had loaded heavy planks on the trucks for inevitable emergencies. These were now needed for crossing three lines of deep trenches, eight feet wide, dug by the defenders of Sian. The passengers, equally wise in the ways of travel, decided to walk. As they all filed through barbed wire entanglements put up by the attacking army, soldiers came running up with encouraging shouts and the warning that one woman and her daughter had almost stepped on a land mine. The soldiers, laughing in anticipation of the deadly surprise for their enemies, pointed out where other mines were hidden and guided the party to safety.

Tungkwan, on the Shensi-Honan border, was filled with soldiers and the tired travelers found no place to spend the night. Even the railroad station was full, but the stationmaster graciously invited the whole party into his own home. His wife quickly prepared bowls of steaming hot rice soup and spread blankets on the stone floor for the comfort of the children. Two rooms were hardly adequate as sleeping quarters for 77 people. The women and some of the men found a place to sit, but Englund and others had the whole night to practice what he called "standing endurance."

The following morning a train pulled in with a special car attached for the refugees. In fact, the car was too special. Because the heat coupling did not fit the rest of the train, it could offer its passengers only refrigerated conditions for the journey to the Coast.

In Shanghai Englund immediately found opportunities for teaching the Scriptures. In his own words, "we have kept quite busy since coming to the Coast. Last week I had five chapel meetings out at the Women's Bible Seminary at Kiangwan, which is a kind of suburb of Shanghai. I have also had several other meetings in different parts of the city. There has also been a lot of treasurer's work to catch up on."

News and rumors from Sian trickled in. Troops of Chiang Kai-shek's Central Government held the city; some of Marshal Chang's forces had turned bandits; Lantien and Huhsien had been looted; young women had been carried off by soldiers; a Bible school graduate had been taken captive; communist troops were near the city—who knew the true story? The hard fact to face was that neither the Chinese authorities nor the U.S. Consulate would permit missionaries to return to Shensi. But Englund's heart was there and with eyes upon God he waited to know His will. He refused furlough believing that he had unfinished work in Sian. He was also concerned about his three daughters. Miriam was ready for college, Grace would graduate from Chefoo the following year and Winifred was ready to begin school. With a quiet smile he turned to his "Golden Queen" who was celebrating her birthday. "The Lord will provide, Anna," he said, "the Lord will certainly provide."

13

Thankful

Whatever the circumstances, William Englund always saw reasons for being thankful to God. Neither personal problems nor China hardships smothered his happy appreciation of blessing from the Lord.

Thankful for a summer reunion with their children in Chefoo where they had the added joy of seeing Grace baptized, William and Anna Englund prepared to return to Sian. To all the routine dangers of travel had been added the threat of bombings. By 1937 Japan had given up all pretense of hiding her ambitions and was determined to force China to bend to her arrogant will. The Englunds arrived by ship in Tsingtao without incident and boarded the train for Tsinan. Chinese army officers graciously gave up their claim to the waiting room so that Englund and his wife, together with three women from the Church Mission, could have exclusive use of the wooden benches and cold stone floor for the night.

The express train early the following morning could not have been more welcome. A connection was made in Hsuchow without delay and the whole trip from Tsingtao to Sian was completed in the incredible time of less than two days. It was enough to make a mule faint with astonishment, but the Englunds had a special reason for thankfulness to God. Had they missed the Hsuchow connection, they would have been in the city when it was mercilessly bombed by Japanese planes. As they praised God for His care, they pleaded that He would show mercy to poor, bleeding China.

His wife spoke for them both when she wrote to T. J. Bach in the Spring of 1937, "Praise God from whom all blessings flow. As you see from the above address we are back HOME." All immediate difficulties had been overcome. Winifred had joined her sisters in school.

The Englunds were back in Sian. The Bible school had been reopened and all students, except two, had returned. Prison officials had asked for evangelistic services to be resumed. As soon as martial law was lifted the city chapel opened its doors every night. The one unhappy note was that nothing could be learned about the young evangelist captured by brigands. His father, Pastor Chang Hsiao-i of the Hsingping church, pleaded with tears for others to join him in prayer, but no news was heard until long after the young man had been given up as lost. His adventures took him to Shanghai where he fought in the Nationalist armies against Japan. He eventually returned home and following in his father's footsteps became a pastor.

There were other causes for thanksgiving. In the Sian West Church alone 59 new believers were baptized and in spite of danger, trouble and hardships facing them, three young TEAM missionaries had dared to leave the security of their homeland for the uncertainties of life in China. No one could read the future, but like the unwavering gleam of a bright star was the fact that Christ's victory at the Cross was irreversible. The day would inevitably come when every knee in China would bow to Him. Meanwhile, Englund was thankful for many local victories as hundreds of people of all classes and ages were swept into the Kingdom through preaching of the gospel. He was thankful also for unlimited opportunities and took a swift look at the calendar. There was, he optimistically believed, time for a quick visit to Lantien.

Other people for different reasons had made the same decision and Englund found himself swallowed up in a crowd struggling to buy bus tickets. Those joining the mob last overcame the handicap of their late arrival by climbing over the heads of others. Englund, with life nearly squeezed out of him, pushed his bleeding hand through the ticket window and bought two tickets. He did not notice that his wrist watch had been torn off in the titanic struggle until a guard came along with a dirty little boy holding the watch and looking for its owner. Thankful to the Lord for such unexpected honesty, Englund rewarded the boy and took back the watch which, he pointed out to his travel companion, "showed less scratches than its owner."

Knowing that Sian would certainly come under air attacks, Englund's first task was to prepare 20-foot deep tunnels at the Bible Institute and Mission premises. With these precautions completed, he turned to other matters. Bible school classes, Field Committee meetings, correspondence, accounts, and consultations with pastors again filled his busy days. A high priority was given to planning an evangelistic campaign for which Dr. John Sung had been invited by the Chinese Church Association.

Dr. Sung's visit to Sian will never be forgotten by those who heard him. Sometimes called the "Billy Sunday of China," he was outstanding even in a land of gifted preachers. Earlier in the year, T. J. Bach had quoted in a letter to Englund, "when the enemy shall come in like a flood, the Spirit of the Lord shall lift up a standard against him," and with keen insight added that the organized forces of darkness continually resist with all their might the work of God's servants. He also encouraged Englund to claim the promised power.

With the coming of John Sung to Sian, God's standard was lifted up and God's power seen in remarkable ways. People crowded into the Sian West Church to hear him preach three or four times a day. Those who could not get into the building stood around the windows, or sat in a large tent connected to the church. The audience sat or stood, silent and still, as John Sung suddenly pulled a tiny wooden coffin from the pocket of his gown. The subject was taking an unpleasant turn. Worse was to come. He began pulling out slips of paper on which were written the names of death-dealing sins.

Another evening, Dr. Sung held up a large sheet of paper, white and unmarked. If anyone was under the delusion that a comfortable message was about to follow, he was quickly surprised. Seizing a flashlight, Sung held it behind the paper and the Chinese character for "sin" appeared, black and accusing. What the speaker illustrated with coffin, paper and flashlight, the Holy Spirit emphasized with overwhelming power. Some who heard fought against God's working and rejected His grace to their loss. They turned their anger against the evangelist who calmly announced one evening that he had received two threats against his life . . . but many responded to the offer of salvation. Over 500 people were counseled in eight days. Some were Christians who needed to get right with God, but the majority were new believers. And on the final day of the campaign 500 sick people were prayed for, many later testifying of their healing.

The Englunds had Dr. Sung as their guest while he was in Sian and they joined a large crowd at the railroad station to bid him a reluctant farewell. As the train pulled out, Sian station echoed with gospel hymns heartily sung. God had lifted up a standard against the enemy, great victories had been won and believers multiplied.

Air raids became more frequent and the underground shelters were used more often. Most of the bombs fell to the west of the city where there was an airfield and army barracks, both uncomfortably close to the Mission premises. Windows of the Bible Institute and the West Side Church were smashed. When Englund looked at some of the craters he noticed uneasily that bombs had penetrated deeper than his 20-foot shelters. Even the dead had been disturbed by the violence of war. Bones were scattered in all directions from graves blown open by explosions. Surveying the desolation he praised God for being both a rock beneath his feet and a shield above his head.

In these war conditions Bible Institute students became restless and nervous, their concentration disturbed by listening instinctively for air raid warnings. Englund reluctantly decided once more to close the school and the regular class was graduated with two years of study completed. He watched them leave one by one, carrying their bundles and books and when the last had gone he turned into the forlorn and empty Bible school. "May the Lord be with them, and make them a blessing wherever He will use them," he prayed softly.

War was coming in all its fury, but Englund was thankful that opportunities for evangelism remained. Looking back over 33 years of service, he was able to write that "there had never been such opportunities for preaching the gospel as now." The Sian circuit of churches reported that nearly 300 people were baptized in 1936. Three days of special meetings in the Sian Independent Church resulted in over 100 decisions for Christ and even from the vast tragedies of war, God marvelously extracted blessings. Among the crowds of refugees seeking safety in the West were many Christians glad to find spiritual homes in Shensi churches, where their gifts and energy added to the total witness for Christ.

Christmas without their children was a lonely experience for the Englunds, their full support was being faithfully and generously provided by the Norwegian Evangelical Free Church in Jersey City and the Salem Evangelical Free Church in Chicago. The Mission home Board had voted $300 for their passage home and Roy Brehm, a close friend and fellow worker, had contacted the Chicago League for the Hard of Hearing for information on lip reading classes . . . but travel wa perilous. Much of the Chinese section of Shanghai was already in ruins, after the heroic stand four years earlier by troops of the 19th Route Army, against Japanese marines supported by naval and air bombardments. Western nations watching Hitler's moves in Europe with increasing alarm had little interest in coming to China's aid. She would soon face her hour of travail alone.

As for most missionaries, furlough suddenly lost its attraction when the time came to say good-by to Chinese friends and fellow Christians. William Englund and his wife began to dread the parting almost as much as they looked forward to reunion with their daughters and their relatives in America. The day rushed upon them. The familiar journey from Sian to Hankow by train was soon completed, but instead of continuing east through the war zone, the Englunds traveled south to Canton. The U.S. Consulate arranged for a third class sleeper to be attached to the Hankow-Canton express, with a large American flag spread over the roof of the car. The sinking of the U.S. gunboat, Panay, by Japanese planes 30 miles above Nanking was not a good omen that the Stars and Stripes would offer much protection, and missionary passengers found more assurance in knowing that they were under the wings of the Almighty. In fact, Japanese planes flew over the train only once, but stops were long and frequent to avoid entering areas being bombed. On the final section from Canton to

Hong Kong, they saw many stretches of road cratered by heavy bombs. When thankfully entering British territory they learned that a devastating air attack on Canton and the railway missed them by only a few hours.

In Hong Kong, Englund was thankful for an invitation to take part in a Bible conference for workers of the Free Church Mission. His Northern Chinese was not understood, but Katherine Tang proved to be an excellent interpreter into Cantonese. Language was no barrier to such great blessing. So he decided to pass up the opportunity to continue the journey to Shanghai with other missionaries. Englund spoke twice a day at the conference and the Lord sent fires of revival down from heaven.

The Canadian Pacific SS Empress of Canada moved sedately from her moorings under the shadow of Hong Kong peak and headed for Shanghai. Listed among the third class passengers were Rev. and Mrs. W. G. Englund, impatient to see their daughters. Excitement drove all other thoughts away, and Anna wrote to a friend, "Last night poor Will and I could hardly get to sleep, most likely due to the excitement of the children's coming." They were not disappointed, although only Miriam and Winifred able to come from Chefoo. Grace remained in school to graduate and was then escorted to the West Coast to join her parents.

Anyone following Englund around Shanghai would have thought that he had forgotten all about furlough. He had daily meetings in Chinese or English. For one week he spoke every morning at the China Inland Mission. The following week he taught daily at a Chinese Bible school. Invitations came from all directions and Englund accepted each one eagerly. It was as if he knew that not much time remained allowing the teaching of God's Word by foreign missionaries in China. A world at war and the falling of the Bamboo Curtain were about to exclude missionaries from a land they loved as their own. But present opportunities were magnificent and Englund was thankful to God that a large party of veteran missionaries were returning to China with 40 recruits.

William and Anna Englund, with Miriam and Winifred, sailed from Shanghai at the end of May, 1938. It was 35 years since he arrived in obedience to a vision which had not dimmed. His first thought aboard the SS Empress of Japan was to send a cable to the Mission office in Chicago: "ARRIVING SEATTLE FIFTEENTH NOTIFY MOTHER." It was the happiest news Mrs. Ida Englund had received in a long time.

14

Persistent

The SS President Cleveland freed of her moorings, eased away from the San Francisco pier. Rev. and Mrs. Englund with four other TEAM missionaries had again broken ties with their own land to face the hardship of another term of service in China. On the dock was Pastor Swenson of the Mission Covenant Church who had seen the very first group of TEAM missionaries sent out many years before. Englund's boyhood neighbors, Mr. and Mrs. Swanson, were there, too, representative of a great number of faithful friends from whom he was parting once more. Their faces grew indistinct as the ship gathered speed, glided under the bridges, passed Treasure Island and the World Fair, and on through the Golden Gate to the open Pacific. It was August 9, 1940. The Englunds had been on furlough two years and two months, but, as when Jacob worked to win his sweetheart Rachel, the time "had seemed but a few days."

Aboard ship Englund looked back over the happy times. God had done so much. A special blessing was to have the exclusive use of the old family home at 2642 East 63rd Street, Seattle, for three months while waiting for Grace to arrive from Chefoo. Two months on the East Coast followed visiting Anna Englund's family. The final year and a half in TEAM's Franson-Risberg Memorial apartment in Chicago had been another provision of the Lord. God had made good His promise to give houses a hundredfold to those who leave home for His sake, and as he thought over his travels in all directions, Englund figured that the number of different beds he had slept in were certainly a hundredfold and more! The pastor of a Norwegian Free Church in Seattle had spoken prophetic words when furlough began. "While the Englunds are here for a time of rest, we must make use of them all we can," he announced to his congregation. In fact, Englund's schedule began to alarm the Mission leaders. Rev. Roy Brehm, in concern wrote, "I was sorry to hear of all the meetings that you are having. I fear for your health, Brother." But the next paragraph of the same letter continued, "Brother Oscar Larsen of Salem here has the oversight of a little church near Chicago, and hopes to have a missionary conference of three days. He is wondering if you will be here at that time, and if so, could you give them several messages?"

God had blessed the family in other ways. Grace and Miriam had been accepted by Wheaton College and the problem of their tuition solved. Winifred had enjoyed her first experience in America, but was looking forward to being back "home" in China, and in school in Chefoo. Personal needs had been met in spite of a general tightness of money. Meticulous in keeping accounts, Englund had made out a statement of receipts and expenses for the first quarter of 1940. Travel expenses over a large area between Chicago and Oregon amounted to $15.50. Gifts received totalled $34.20, leaving a balance of $18.70 to be credited to his account. Anna also had a small credit item. She had carefully put to one side an envelope containing 15 single dollar bills. In the rush of packing the envelope had been thrown into the wastepaper basket where it was discovered by young John Christiansen. After the finder had been rewarded and a few C.O.D. charges paid $1.94 remained.

Financial support had been promised in full and Englund took out his typewriter to make a list of those who were committed to share in his ministry. He had hardly begun when a ship's notice was posted advising passengers of a one hour deadline for mail to the U.S. Englund hurriedly made a second start using the same heading but arranging the names differently. By mistake both lists were sent off and in a letter of apology to Siri Malmstrom at TEAM headquarters, Englund wrote, "It must have appeared puzzling to you, and no wonder at that, because any creature with two heads would look strange."

As the SS President Cleveland settled into its ocean stride, passengers tried to find their sea legs, some with more success than others. But when the ship turned south to Hawaii, the Pacific relaxed and life aboard became pleasant. It was difficult to realize that on the other side of the world Hitler's army and air force had already smashed into Poland, swallowed up Czechoslovakia and turned ruthlessly against Holland, Belgium, England and France. The fields of Flanders were again red with blood and, secretly, in Japan, navy pilots were daily practicing for a deadly attack on Pearl Harbor. When the ship docked in Honolulu nothing suggested that land, sea and sky would soon be full of the sounds and horrors of war. Sweet smelling leis and a traditional "Aloha" welcomed passengers to the sunny, peaceful islands.

Conditions in Japan, however, were ominous. Ruth Forsberg, later to become a TEAM missionary, met the Englunds in Yokohama with a warning that to point at anything in the streets would be regarded with suspicion and might easily lead to a police inquiry. Oppresive gloom hung over the Land of the Rising Sun. Prices were high and sugar rationed to one half pound per person per month. The Imperial Army had a stranglehold on national affairs and made its presence felt everywhere. Passengers on the President Cleveland silently watched her cargo of scrap iron, tin and cotton being unloaded. But even they could not guess that within a few months that same metal might come raining down as bombs on the U.S. Fleet in Pearl Harbor. A typhoon lashed their ship as they sailed from Japan. The fury of the adverse wind was like a gigantic warning of devastation about to be loosed in the Pacific. Describing the experience, Englund wrote to T. J. Bach, "It was real rough for a time. My poor Anna had to retire at about 3:00 p.m., but did not get really sick. A number of passengers were kept from the dining room last night and some were sick in earnest." Mrs. Englund, apparently, did not put her heart into it!

Shanghai's familiar sights came into view and as he went ashore Englund suddenly remembered that it was 37 years almost to the day that he had first landed in China. A "very good and blessed time from God" began immediately. Invitations to preach both to Chinese and English-speaking congregations poured in, and as God's servant ministered in the power of the Holy Spirit, revival fell like refreshing dew before the heat of a summer day. It was fresh evidence that regardless of the turmoil in China, God's promise remained valid, "I know the thoughts that I think towards you . . . thoughts of peace and not of evil, to give you an expected end."

With Winifred safely in school, the Englunds put all their energies into preparation for the complicated journey to Sian. When Englund first traveled inland in 1903 conditions had been difficult. In 1940 problems were so enormous that U.S. Government officials and many friends in Shanghai advised against returning to Shensi. A warm invitation from the Shanghai Bible Seminary to teach there for six months was an attractive alternative. "But the Lord urged us to go," Englund wrote to his prayer partners. "Trustingly we could commit both the difficult way before us as well as our little Winifred in Chefoo to His loving care. There 'the sparrow hath found a house, and the swallow a nest,' and both are safe in His keeping."

If the Englunds could have reached their destination as easily and quickly as a swallow flies to her nest, they would have been thrilled. In fact, between them and Sian was an unfriendly Japanese army, guerrilla bands, a flooded no man's land and loyal Chinese troops engaged in the raging battle. Railroad tracks and tunnels had been bombed and all forms of transportation dislocated by war. To complete the journey they would need a Japanese steamer, trains, a bus, wheelbarrows, carts, river boats, a barge and rickshaws. Nothing less than the love of Christ could give them persistence to face such difficulties.

The voyage from Shanghai to Tsingtao was smooth and pleasant until Japanese health officers detected cholera germs on some passengers and put the ship in quarantine for 24 hours. The area was under Japanese control although Chinese guerrillas often blew up railroad tracks and trains. Thankful to God for His protection, the Englunds rested at the Southern Baptist Mission home in Kweiteh but were dismayed to learn that missionaries there were about to leave for the Coast on the advice of their consulate. Yet God opened the door for travel in the opposite direction. After examining all the baggage, Japanese officials quickly issued a permit for the journey by bus to Pochow, their last outpost. Soldiers there allowed them to move into no man's land, where they exchanged the relative comfort of the bus for a contraption vaguely described as a cart. It consisted of two narrow boards between well-patched rickshaw wheels. For the benefit of the puller and discomfort of the passenger, baggage was nicely balanced at each end of the planks. The center space was too short for any man. The only solution was to place both feet on one pile of baggage and rest head and back against the opposite pile. The cart tilted up considerably at the front end when pulled, so that experienced travelers found it best to ride facing backwards. As Englund climbed aboard and adjusted to the unusual position, he remarked to Anna that he felt like a "new moon." With their traveling companions, the Earl Petersons, they endured 20 miles of this novel form of transportation before reaching a watery waste.

In their determination to hold back a Japanese advance, the Chinese had opened the Yellow River dikes, flooding vast areas of fertile land. Farmers had become fishermen, some casting nets outside their homes. Villages on higher ground were little islands. Everywhere yellow, muddy water swirled. China was fighting for her life at incredible cost and brave, persistent missionaries were willing to suffer with her.

Renting a small boat, the versatile travelers found that a new contortion was necessary. The "new moons" assumed the shape of pancakes. After all baggage had been put aboard, the four passengers were shown the cabin. It was six feet square on the floor and no more than three feet high, and served a multipurpose. At the beginning of the day it was a house of prayer where the Lord of glory met with His faithful servants. Then it became a kitchen. The two men took a mini-walk on the mini-deck while their wives rolled up the bedding and cooked breakfast on a kerosene stove. When the food was passed out of the hatch, Englund remarked that it was the best automat he had ever seen and did not cost a nickel. As evening came, the cabin became a bedroom where the four passengers, wearing their day clothes, squeezed in. The boat was poled over the flood waters, except when they reached old dikes, where the crew clambered ashore to haul their

99

craft with long ropes. Occasionally everyone enjoyed the luxury of being gently wafted along by a favorable breeze strong enough to fill a quickly hoisted sail. Broken bridges and water too shallow even for their flatbottomed boats at times caused delays. After floating triumphantly through the main streets of many villages, their craft like Noah's ark eventually rested on dry land, but torrential rain quickly turned the area into a sea of mud.

The Englunds and Petersons transferred themselves and their baggage to wheelbarrows for the three mile stretch to the Sha River, but were soon bogged down. Animals hitched to farm wagons came to the rescue, hauling them to a waiting wood burning steam launch and barge. Each couple was assigned a private room, although Englund could not help noticing that "the state of the staterooms was far from stately." They could, however, take a sponge bath and change clothes for the first time in many days. The luxury cruise lasted only a day. They then reverted to the "new moon" position on carts. Missionary persistence in reaching a God-given objective was matched by Chinese ingenuity and doggedness. The multipatched tires on Englund's cart were forever blowing out with noisy explosions sending clouds of dust flying in all directions, but each time the patient coolie produced a new patch and cheerfully made repairs. Travel weary, they were glad to see, at last, the old city of Loyang and breathe the air of Free China. From there to Sian the railway was in Chinese hands but under Japanese gunfire. When the Englunds climbed out of the train at the entrance to a tunnel smashed by a heavy Japanese bombardment, they were delighted to see a familiar Chinese face. Julius Bergstrom had thoughtfully sent someone to meet them, and to help them over the 15-mile section where a connecting train was waiting. Because part of the road was within range of enemy guns they waited for the protective cover of night. In total darkness, they filed silently through the bomb-blasted city of Tungkuan. Death from the skies daily hurled countless Chinese into eternity. If ever there was urgent need to point men and women to the Savior it was now. China in her hour of agony desperately needed God and William and Anna Englund, struggling with all the hardships and perils of the bleeding land they loved so much, rejoiced that the Lord had called them back for "such a time as this." For them it was to be, in Churchill's famous phrase, "their finest hour."

Boarding the train on the other side of the tunnel, they arrived safely in Sian shortly after midnight. They had taken 57 days to travel the 750 miles from Shanghai. Englund spoke for everyone when he said, "All glory to our heavenly Father for His loving care and unchanging faithfulness." No one had suffered injury or sickness; nothing had been lost. A cable received at Mission headquarters in Chicago read, "ENGLUND PETERSONS ARRIVED SIAN." It did not tell the whole story.

In no area of his life was Englund more persistent than in prayer and preaching. After a pleasant Christmas with Rev. and Mrs. Bergstrom, Englund, like a giant refreshed, was ready for the new year. The pace was breathtaking. A week of evangelism in the Sian Gospel Hall was followed by seven days of classes for Chinese workers. Then came a week of Bible study, prayer, evangelistic services and conference in Lantien. After a few days at home, he was off again. A sleepless night waiting for a train, two hours on board and a full day by mule cart was needed to reach Pucheng for a conference. On the return journey a choking dust storm delayed the train so much that it probably broke a record of some kind by taking all night to cover 40 miles. To Englund the time seemed longer. The only resting place he could find was the bare wooden frame of what had been a third class upper berth sleeper. His cheerful comment was that "he did not mind being put on the shelf. It was better than having to stand."

In comparison the trip to Sangchen was luxurious. The train journey was without delay and Rev. Reuben Gustafson proudly met him at the station with his rubber-tired, covered, gospel cart, powered by two cows. To this ancient means of travel had been added the latest in communication devices, a loud-speaker. Englund was delighted. His ears were almost useless, but his powerful voice was boosted to reach multitudes. Like battle-tested warriors riding to fresh victories, Englund and Gustafson triumphantly moved from revival in Sangchen to Hsingping. The speed of the gospel cart was not great, and they could never be sure that Japanese planes would not strafe them in the mistaken belief that they were carrying supplies to the front.

Englund was in Hsingping a month, teaching complete courses in what was called a short term Bible school. There were 80 eager students. Englund also found time to attend prayer meetings, assist at regular church services, and take his turn in preaching to large crowds with the help of the loud-speaker. On Palm Sunday his message on Christ's entry into Jerusalem reached the ears of a man in the post office in the next street and struck him with such conviction that he hurried to the church, seeking the Savior. During the month there were at least 100 public decisions for Christ. While men made war, God was offering peace through faith in His Son, and "to them that sat in the region and shadow of death, to them did light spring up."

It is not surprising that when Englund returned home he confessed to being "somewhat exhausted physically and needing a rest before speaking in the missionary union prayer meeting and then in a four-day Chinese conference in our Sian Church." God again met his needs. Many turned to Christ and 30 believers were baptized. Englund was so refreshed that he was more than ready for a similar conference in Lantien. His eagerness somehow communicated itself to the mule pulling the cart in which he and his fellow worker, Mr. Hsieh, were comfortably seated. Breaking with tradition, the animal began to run. With the assist of a downhill grade the mule threw off its driver and left him far behind. The two passengers hung on grimly, hoping that the pace would slacken. But the mule was in a record breaking mood and dashed down the hill with increased speed. Acceleration was its downfall. With a spectacular somersault, the animal bounced off its head and landed crosswise between the shafts. Englund managed to hold on tightly enough not to follow the mule's acrobatics and lost only his hat. Everything else in the cart went flying, but nothing was broken, not even the neck of the mule, which resumed pulling operations with more caution. Lantien rejoiced again to see their beloved missionary-pastor and rejoiced even more at blessings poured out upon them. Christians were renewed, sinners converted and 19 believers baptized.

In spite of heroic effort by the Chinese post office, mail moved precariously under war conditions. Missionaries in the Northwest were in danger of being isolated from their headquarters and packages from the homelands could not reach them. Sitting at his desk, Englund considered the problem. In the typewriter was an urgent letter to "beloved Brother Bach." His "Radio Ear" was on strike and refused to give a single sound. Great progress had been made in the quality of hearing aids, but nothing kept pace with the deterioration of Englund's hearing. In answer to prayer, Mr. and Mrs. Charles Notson of the Christian and Missionary Alliance walked into the office. They were on their way to America and glad to take the letter and hearing aid along. Englund hurriedly concluded his letter. "You have always been so good to us, so we are sure you will gladly do this service also to help the 'earthen vessel without ears.' Thank you for all your kindness and God bless you in return."

He knew that months would pass before the device could be repaired and returned, and minimal hearing restored. His lip reading lessons were of no value in Chinese conversations. Any sound in Chinese can be pronounced in four separate tones, each with an entirely different meaning. Since lip formation is the same for all four tones, a deaf man cannot distinguish between the various meanings.

Preaching was no problem. Englund's voice was strong and clear. His wife was "volume controller," giving signs to indicate that he was speaking too loudly, at too high a pitch, or too quietly. For almost 30 years their perfect understanding kept Englund effectively preaching the Word of God. Many who heard him never knew the secret of his voice control.

Englund's habit was to begin his letters with a Scripture verse and his choices in 1941 reflect conditions that year. He quoted "The eternal God is thy refuge and underneath are the everlasting arms," "In the secret place of the Most High," "Under the shadow of the

Almighty," and "My refuge and my fortress." Sian, whose strong walls were a sanctuary against marauding armies and robber bands, had become a prime target for Japanese bombers, which Anna Englund cautiously referred to in one of her letters home as "birds in the air." The Gospel Hall, where hundreds had accepted Christ, was in ruins. It seemed as if the Devil was determined to destroy every center of life and light. The house where Miss Anna Jensen, a TEAM missionary, lived with a Chinese Bible woman, was a pile of broken bricks, tiles, wood, furniture and crockery. The two women had escaped death by the miracle of God's protection. In the rubble, Miss Jensen found an unbroken picture of Christ the Good Shepherd holding a lamb in His arms. It seemed symbolic. Amid the constant thunder of crashing bombs, Englund had little time to write. Contact with friends was made through what he called "the Heavenly Central" where he made daily calls "ringing with praise and with prayer for the fullness of God's blessing." The more bombs came down, the more prayer went up.

Fifty years had passed since the first 35 TEAM missionaries had arrived in China, sped on their way with the promise,

> "But now thus saith the Lord that created thee, O Jacob, and He that formed thee, O Israel, Fear not: for I have redeemed thee, I have called thee by thy name; thou art mine. When thou passest through the waters, I will be with thee; and through the rivers, they shall not overflow thee: when thou walkest through the fire, thou shalt not be burned; neither shall the flame kindle upon thee."

At the Golden Jubilee, 41 TEAM missionaries were in China and all could testify that God had magnificently kept His promise. With tears and laughter they recounted old memories. Through half a century of endless war, drought, famine, disease, chaos and turmoil, God had miraculously built His Church on the eternal foundation of His Son. Incredible difficulties had been overcome in the name of the Lord Most High. Thousands of Chinese had been delivered from the power of darkness and brought into the light and security of God's kingdom. As they thought on these things, Englund and his fellow missionaries were loud in their songs of praise. It never entered their minds that only ten years remained to finish the work God had given them to do in China.

15

Victorious in Faith

In the decade beginning in 1940 the faith of God's people in China was tested to the limit by crisis after crisis, revolving around such basic issues as daily food, personal safety and family needs. Shensi, deeply scarred by years of bitter fighting, was lashed with the full fury of war. Relentless bombing was part of each day's routine. Millions of Chinese, as if inoculated against despair, improvised, repaired, worked, struggled, laughed, fought and died.

Churches, sharing in the common suffering, were alert to their golden opportunity and reaped a harvest in Christ's name. Rocketing prices robbed money of its value. Missionaries dependent on funds from America grappled with the problem of a more or less fixed income, a fixed rate of exchange, and an uncontrolled cost of living. The problem was not accounts and bookkeeping, but daily bread. Englund, entering long rows of expense figures in Chinese dollars, was keenly aware of an inadequate income in U.S. dollars. It was, he wrote, "the greatest trial of faith in the history of the Mission." Wheat cost the equivalent of $40 (U.S.) a bushel, and coal $200 (U.S.) a ton.

Prayer and extreme economy were the only solution. The Englunds learned that to pray, "Give us this day our daily bread," was not a mere formula to recite but an exercise of faith. They were encouraged by T. J. Bach's remark, "If ends do not meet, put God in between." Answers to prayer came often through the generosity of Chinese Christians who themselves were suffering great hardship. Eggs and bread brought to missionary homes were thankfully received and Englund's tender heart was touched when Chinese believers offered to pay his travel expenses as he toured the district teaching God's Word.

Practical economies were many. When the price of coal went sky-high, the Englunds lived in their kitchen so that the precious fuel could both keep them warm and cook their food. As Anna prepared the evening meal, William sat at a little table writing to prayer partners. "Our meals come hot from the stove and this letter also comes warm from both kitchen and a heart filled with praise and prayer," he wrote. Milk and butter were written off as impossible luxuries. In earlier days the Englunds had owned a cow which was fed with soy-beans to enrich and increase her milk. Now they by-passed the cow and made substitute milk direct from the beans. The product looked remarkably like milk, but tasted remarkably different.

Inflation made travel difficult. Journeys by bus or mule cart cost more than a missionary budget allowed, but the Lord's command to go and preach the gospel was not conditional, to be set aside during economic crises. Englund, already past his 60th birthday, and affectionately known to countless Chinese Christians as "old pastor," took to a bicycle. He had considered his years too many for such an exercise, but discovered that "the Lord who gave the prophet Elisha's dead bones life restoring power could also give sufficient strength to my old legs for the turning of wheels in His blessed service." Speed was sacrificed, but not obedience. The effort was never in vain. After cycling 20 miles across the Sian plain in intense heat for several days of conference with Chinese officials, Englund saw an influential Buddhist converted. When bedding had to be carried for an overnight stay, travel by bicycle was impossible and Englund was forced to the alternatives of riding a donkey or using Reuben Gustafson's gospel wagon, drawn by faithful cows. Attacks by enemy planes added to other difficulties, but gave unusual opportunities. On one occasion, Englund and a Chinese believer, hiding behind a wall from a strafing run by a fighter plane, witnessed to a man with them in the ditch and led him to Christ.

No solution could be found to the problem of reopening the Bible Institute. Funds for a Chinese staff did not exist and students had no financial help. Constant bombing of Sian discouraged new students entering the school, and would have made regular teaching impossible. Englund, in faith, committed to God "the Bible school question and all other problems in the work and there our burdens rest," and turned with fresh enthusiasm and energy to Bible teaching and evangelism in the Sian district. The thunder of war had not disturbed his deep conviction that the gospel "is the power of God unto salvation," and he continued to trust the Holy Spirit for results.

Because of travel costs, he could not take Anna with him, and sometimes started out with smoke already billowing from bombed houses and knowing that before he returned other ruthless attacks would follow. He confessed that the situation was "nerve-racking" but clung tightly to the promise that the eternal God was his refuge.

Trusting the Lord to protect his wife, Englund continued to ride his bicycle to conference after conference. Sometimes he was away from home one week, occasionally two.

He prepared carefully so that he was always able to preach or teach a complete subject or cover a book in the time allotted. The whole Bible was his textbook. In Sian he daily taught the book of Acts, refusing to stop when Japanese bombers were circling the city. At another Sian church, started in the north of the city by a businessman, he taught the entire Epistle to the Ephesians in seven days. In Kienhsien he spoke on the second Epistle to Timothy; in Hsingping he concentrated on the theme of "The hand of the Lord was upon Ezekiel;" and at another conference led a series of studies on the life of Samuel. For two days of special services in a small church ten miles from Sian, he decided to teach part of the Epistle to the Romans.

After a day of sickness which kept him in bed, he rode out on his bicycle. Near his destination, roads and fields were under water from heavy rains. Two men from the church were waiting, one to carry the bicycle through the water, and the other to carry the rider. Halfway across, the man carrying Englund stepped into a deep hole and momentarily both of them disappeared. Englund was so wet that it would have made no difference if he had waded ashore, but the Christian brother was determined to finish what he had begun and cheerfully insisted on carrying his beloved missionary-pastor, now doubly heavy from his saturated clothes. Englund had nothing to change into and stayed wet most of the day. "But such a chilling experience did not dampen the message which the Lord gave me to deliver in two blessed meetings that day. The chapel was filled with people and the Lord's presence warmed our hearts," he wrote afterwards. There was, however, a physical price to pay. His right arm was in almost unbearable arthritic pain day and night for a week.

No conference was without blessing and many conferences received a special blessing. A typical phrase in Englund's reports is, "Best of all was our experience of the Lord's presence." Chinese and missionaries together learned to trust God in new ways. At the beginning of one conference all the bread was spread out before the Lord with a prayer that He would keep it from going moldy as long as services continued. The answer exceeded their asking. Food was preserved in excellent condition and was so abundant that grateful Chinese were glad to share with Englund a substantial gift of eggs.

To the trial of faith through high food prices, limited finance and the perils of war was added a new and terrible element when Japan launched her surprise attack on Pearl Harbor. The conflict in Asia took on a fresh aspect. The United States and China became allies and all Americans on territory occupied by Japan were arrested and put in concentration camps. Japanese military authorities confiscated the China Inland Mission school in Chefoo and moved staff and students to the Presbyterian Mission on Temple Hill where a large number of other people were interned. Crowding was so bad there that as many as 20 persons shared a room.

Without desks, equipment or beds, and with teachers and pupils divided at random into three groups, it seemed impossible that classes could continue. Some of the less studious took the optimistic view that the outbreak of war had brought lessons to an end, but they had underestimated the ingenuity of the staff. Teachers in each group prepared to teach all subjects, even if they were only one lesson ahead of their students. A paper shortage was overcome by using every inch of every margin of every page. Children sat and slept on the floor, and school continued so effectively that when the students finally returned to their homeland, they were a year ahead of their grades.

All of this was unknown to William and Anna Englund in Sian. They always felt intensely the emotional strain of being separated from their children, but previously had felt consoled knowing that in an emergency they could somehow or other get to Chefoo. Now they were separated from their daughter by impenetrable battle lines. Japan's imperial army, determined to bend all Asia to its proud will, stood between them and their Winifred. They constantly reminded each other that God's promise of being able to keep that which is committed unto Him included their daughter, and one day, like a gleam of sunshine, came a telegram from the China Inland Mission in Shanghai, "CHEFOO CHILDREN SEND LOVE PARENTS ALL WELL HAPPY."

Contact by mail was briefly made, but the secret channel soon closed and efforts through the International Red Cross were without success. Far away in Switzerland the United States was negotiating with Japan through the Swiss Consul for an exchange of nationals. Rumors reached Sian that a Japanese ship would take Americans from China to a port in Portuguese East Africa where an American ship would be waiting. Both ships, of course, would face the danger of being sunk.

In a chaotic world only God was absolutely trustworthy, and William and Anna Englund turned to Him again. In a letter which he hoped might miraculously reach its destination, Englund wrote, "We are glad that the highest route of communication remains open in spite of war and disturbances on earth. Remember our telephone number is always Ephesians 6:18, 19 — "Praying always with all prayer and supplication in the Spirit and watching thereunto with all perseverance and supplication for all saints; and for me, that utterance may be given unto me, that I may open my mouth boldly, to make known the mystery of the gospel."

Finally rumor became fact, prayer became praise, and faith was confirmed. The Englunds learned with joy that Winifred had safely arrived in America on the SS Gripsholm and was with relatives. She had found a letter from her parents when the ship called at Goa. It had been mailed in the belief that God would make sure it would be delivered.

In the summer of 1944, the Japanese resumed their offensive in China and Sian was crowded with refugees. Every mission home in the city was filled with missionaries driven westward by advancing armies. Shensi province had not been penetrated, but the threat of invasion daily grew more alarming. Englund had spent the first half of the year in an unbroken succession of Bible classes, district conferences, special meetings and evangelism. Only a visit to Kienhsien remained to complete his schedule. With the war situation so critical he hesitated to make the trip, but had learned long before that to wait for favorable circumstances was to wait forever ... so he went, tenderly committing his wife to God's safe keeping. The first day of conference had not ended when he was urgently recalled to Sian by telephone and telegraph. Borrowing an old Chinese bicycle with a broken spring, he started out immediately on the 50 mile ride. At Lichuan he was able to exchange the ancient machine for a better one loaned to him by a fellow missionary, Miss Edith Johnson. A strong wind against him, scorching sun above him, and a hilly road beneath him were so exhausting that he had to struggle part way on foot, the bicycle being wheeled at his side. Praying and trusting God for strength, he reached Hsienyang moments before the Sian train pulled out. With thankful heart, he clambered into the baggage car, bicycle and all.

The situation in Sian was critical. The American Embassy had advised all U.S. citizens to leave immediately. A meeting of the TEAM Field Committee was hurriedly called and, like King Hezekiah when faced with the threat of war, they placed the matter before the Lord. The answer seemed clear to all. Older missionaries and those not in good health should join a large party of workers from other missions due to leave in a few days and the young and strong should stay on as long as possible, prepared to escape by bicycle at any moment.

The Englunds faced again a conflict of emotions peculiar to missionary life. They were about to leave Chinese brothers and sisters whom they loved as dearly as their own family and they looked forward to reunion with their dearly loved children, relatives and friends. They would be free from the strain, suffering and dangers of China, but they would be separated from places where they had seen God do mighty wonders.

Missionaries have sometimes been accused of imposing their own culture on other nations. In China the opposite was more often true. Missionaries were gently and imperceptibly overcome by the fascinations of Chinese art, poetry, humor, architecture, improvisation, culture and cooking. With non-Christian religion and practices there was no compromise, but generous hospitality, genuine and lasting friendship, and, above all, practical love shown in a thousand ways by Chinese who knew Christ, was irresistable. Many became more Chinese than Western in their ways. None of this made parting from Christian friends easy.

For three days Sian was a scene of frantic activity. God confirmed the decision to leave China by leading to the Englunds a high ranking Chinese officer who helped them to quickly sell their few possessions and arranged transportation to the railroad station. Pressed as they were for time, Englund managed to give two full days to a Sian church conference in fulfillment of his promise. Then came his final Sunday in the city. The climax of a farewell service was the gift of a pennant, with an embroidered heart in the center and on it the Chinese character for love.

When the Englunds said good-by to a crowd of friends at the railroad station, they never guessed that it would be four and a half months before they reached their destination. A train took them to the end of the line where buses were generously provided by the Bank of China for the section of the journey to Chengtu, Szechuan province. Englund's northern accent was quickly recognized by local people, but their speech peculiarities fell on his deaf ears. Three weeks later a U.S. army airforce plane flew them to Kunming, capital of Yunnan province. New regulations for persons leaving China threatened to delay their departure for India until the air fares were paid. Englund cut the red tape with prayer, and soon he and his wife were in Calcutta.

Memories of an uncomfortable night under the leaky roof of an old Chinese inn were revived as Englund climbed into his upper berth on the Bombay express. When torrential monsoon rain began dripping in, he reached for his umbrella and with veteran skill kept himself dry. Two months in Bombay were happily spent sharing in the work of the Swedish Hindustani Mission. With the help of an interpreter, Englund was able to preach at Sunday services.

The transport which finally arrived to take them back to the United States was carrying thousands of troops as well as hundreds of civilians, most of them missionaries. Mrs. Englund shared a cabin with 17 other women; her husband, more privileged, was in a cabin with only 11 men. The five week voyage was a time of "blessed fellowship," daily devotions, and three Sunday services attended by many of the troops. When San Diego came in sight, Englund's eyes were misty with tears. The Lord had brought him and his wife safely over land and sea, and through the air. Weeks of travel had been enjoyed with opportunities to speak for Christ. God had faithfully fulfilled His promise to keep that which was committed to Him. Sea gulls, swirling in intricate patterns over the stern of the ship, called to those with ears to hear that God rules the world, not guns, and that the heavenly

Father's loving-kindness is without end. The prayers of many friends had been answered. By the grace of God, William and Anna Englund were home again.

Miriam and Grace were eagerly waiting for them in Seattle and in Chicago, Winifred was counting the days anticipating her parents arrival. She was now fourteen and four years had passed since she had seen them. She had been absolutely sure of their daily prayers for her. A flow of letters had come, many mailed when the possibility of delivery was small, but Winifred was a little worried that she might not recognize her parents and asked her uncle, Herman Swenson, to accompany her to the railroad station to meet the West Coast express. She need not have been anxious. Love sees past all superficial changes and instinctively recognizes its own. The reunion was a taste of Heaven.

China, bleeding and exhausted, was forced to her knees but not defeated. Her soldiers, poorly armed and underfed, fought stubborn rear guard actions as they slowly retreated westward before steady pressure from the Japanese. Except for the extreme southwest, most of the vast country fell to the enemy, but behind Japanese lines Chinese guerrillas blew up bridges, and railroad tracks.

Their ingenuity was unlimited. Chinese sailors, disguised as coolies, hid on a river bank until one of their homemade mines sank a Japanese naval vessel. Under cover of darkness, they recovered scrap from the wrecked ship and carried it back to their secret factory to make more mines.

War had spread like an uncontrolled forest fire. Hong Kong had been attacked and occupied. Burma jungles were the scene of bloody fighting. The tropical islands of the Philippines were filled with the thunder of cannon and bursting bombs. Throughout the blue Pacific ships and planes were playing a deadly game of hide and seek, but the tide of war was turning. It had begun with the arrival in China of General Chennault's famed Flying Tigers who swept China skies clear of deadly bombers. Gradually the mighty military machine of the United States and her allies blocked all Japanese advances and crushed her fighting power. Finally, in a split-second of death and agony Hiroshima and Nagasaki were obliterated by atomic bombs. Japan surrendered. All China was free again. Eight years of suffering and struggle had not been in vain. On August 15, 1945 the miraculous news was flashed across the land that war had ended in victory for China.

16

Obedient to the Vision

For Englund, as long as strength and opportunity remained, God's call to serve Him in China was faithfully obeyed. All through his long career he could say that he was not disobedient to the heavenly vision. By the fall of 1947 he was ready to return again. More than two years had passed since their hurried departure from Shensi, but in heart and prayer the Englunds had never left their beloved province. Morning by morning Englund had risen at dawn, or earlier, to meet with God and "wrestle with principalities and powers of darkness." He had the encouragement that the work was God's, that the spiritual battle for China could be fought as easily in America as in Sian and that an irreversible and decisive victory had already been won at the Cross.

During furlough, the Englunds enjoyed the special blessing of a cozy apartment at the Mission headquarters in Chicago. For Winifred it was the longest time she had been with her parents since leaving Sian for school years earlier, but the pleasant arrangement moved swiftly to an end. "Soon the temporary home will again be broken up, but the happy time we have had here will remain a grateful memory," Englund wrote.

Traveling much and preaching often, he tried to visualize new conditions in China. Prices there had risen so alarmingly that missionary support was three times the prewar level, and those returning were finding it cheaper to take furniture, food and equipment with them. Englund still needed $1,500 a year to meet the minimum set by the Mission, but he was encouraged by God's words to Joshua, "Be strong and of good courage; for the Lord thy God is with thee withersoever thou goest. Prepare you victuals; for ye shall pass over to possess the land."

Letters from Chinese friends urged him to return to Shensi as soon as possible, adding that opportunities for winning men and women to Christ were better than ever. But the strongest urging was from the Lord Himself. Like Paul in Athens, Englund was stirred in spirit with compassion for those in dark ignorance of God's grace and love. He was already 65, but "with glad expectations was preparing once more to return to our China field." By September, 1947 all needs had been met and for the sixth time William Englund stepped ashore in Shanghai.

Accommodations aboard ship had been less spacious than on his first Pacific crossing 44 years earlier. The only available passages were on a troopship with quarters even more cramped than they had been on the voyage from Bombay. Anna had a bunk bed in a cabin with 26 women and children; Englund shared his with "17 other perspiring men." In the middle berth of three, he was thankful to be small enough to be able to turn over, and even to kneel and pray without bumping into the man above him. Typhoon winds of 150 miles an hour off the Philippines and intense heat added to the discomforts of the voyage, but when the weather cleared, the Englunds and ten other TEAM missionaries formed a prayer circle on deck, and found the Lord in their midst. Looking up into the clear blue sky, Englund was reminded of Peter in prayer on a roof top in Joppa and a fresh vision of what God was about to do in China came before him.

The immediate problem was to reach Sian. The end of World War II had not brought peace to China. A new and deadly struggle had surfaced which would be fought to its bitter end. Chiang Kai-shek, faced with the immense task of repairing a vast land devastated by war, was keenly aware of his authority being challenged by Mao Tse-tung and other communist leaders whose troops had been trained and battle-hardened by guerrilla activities against the Japanese. Tough and resolute, they were determined that China should be red.

To the Englunds it seemed as if travel between Shanghai and Sian was normally abnormal. After two weeks of almost daily efforts to clear their baggage through customs, they were told that communist guerrillas had cut the railroad to Sian in several places. "In critical conditions and perplexing times," wrote Englund, "we are thrown much more upon Him, and are brought into closer prayer contact with Himself, and so we thank God for it all."

General Chennault, helping to build a new China after his fighter squadrons returned to the United States, had organized a freight service with a small fleet of veteran DC-3s and DC-4s. He kindly arranged to fly a party of missionaries to Sian at bargain rates and in record time, William and Anna Englund were home again within the high walls of the ancient city. A thousand things needed to be done immediately. Their old house urgently needed repair from war damage. Conferences already planned expected him as special speaker. Opportunities for evangelism had to be grasped. Prayer was both a privilege and a daily necessity for he had "the care of all the churches" in his heart. The Bible Institute, however, was no longer his responsibility. With wise foresight it had been changed into a coeducational vocational Bible school and in preparation for possible radical changes in China, put under a completely Chinese administration. Disturbing rumors of war were prevalent always, as chilling as the cold damp winds sweeping through Shensi, numbing the fingers of Englund as he struggled to make the old house into a cozy home once more. He found encouragement in the prophetic words of Christ, "Ye shall hear of wars and rumors of wars. Be not troubled. This gospel *shall be* preached."

In spite of tense, uncertain conditions, 1948 was the best of all his many years of evangelism. In one place, heavy rains began to fall on the first day of the campaign. A few Christians met, disappointed that the weather had kept almost everyone at home. An amplifier and loud-speaker were a frustrating reminder of their high hopes of reaching thousands with the gospel, but as rain fell persistently day after dreary day, Englund and the evangelistic team felt a growing burden for the area. The harder and longer the rain fell, the harder and longer they prayed. On the final day of the aborted campaign the weather suddenly improved so much that crowds soon gathered to listen to messages carried in all directions by the loud-speaker. By the end of the day more than 50 people had accepted Christ, each one being personally counseled.

That same year, the Sian and Lantien churches baptized about 100 new members and many others accepted Christ. Encouragements were everywhere. Even accidents proved to be for the furtherance of the gospel. One day as Englund and a fellow worker neared Lantien by car, they were stopped by a crowd at a wooden bridge over a gully. A truck, loaded with artillery shells, on which a maximum number of passengers had been nonchalantly sitting, had gone off the road and was lying upside down in a stream at the bottom of the ravine. Injured people were scattered along the bank. Englund offered to take the worst cases to the nearest hospital, and while they were being carried to the car, he used the amplifier to speak of life and salvation in Christ.

In a new phase of the spiritual battle for Shensi, Englund hurried from place to place with the same happy enthusiasm as he had shown 45 years earlier. He could echo Caleb's testimony, "I wholly followed the Lord my God . . . and now, behold, the Lord hath kept me alive these forty and five years . . . as my strength was then, even so is my strength now, for war, both to go out and to come in." In that busy year he was involved in 13 evangelistic campaigns and taught at 16 Bible conferences. Some 11 days were spent with Christian students of Northwest University and a full week with Chinese representatives from the whole area served by The Evangelical Alliance Mission, speaking twice daily on the II Corinthian epistle.

The unseen powers of darkness do not easily surrender their slaves. Counterattacks were inevitable. The war between Japan and China had been over economic issues. Japan had dreamed of a "Greater Asia Co-prosperity Sphere" in which she would have the dominant role. A new war within China was approaching its climax. The issue was philosophic and religious. Communism with its three basic laws, that there is no God, that man is the product of his economic environment and that man is matter in motion, describable in terms of physics and chemistry, was determined to draw all China into its snare. Chiang Kai-shek's armies, exhausted by World War II, were being squeezed south, and their hold upon the Northwest made precarious. During ten days in his favorite city of Lantien, Englund noticed an uneasiness among the people coming for Bible teaching. He did not know that, as in many other cities, communists were already secretly assigned and waiting to take over every official position. On the final day, a missionary suddenly arrived by motorcycle with a warning that the Nationalists had suffered a severe reverse and Sian was in imminent danger of falling into communist hands. He hurried home to help with emergency preparations which were abandoned when the situation improved. But it was not for long.

Two days before Christmas, 1948 and less than a year since returning to Sian, William and Anna Englund were boarding the Lutheran Mission plane, St. Paul, to fly to Canton. Forced out by advancing communists, they would never see Shensi again. Englund had finished the work which the Lord had given him to do in that part of China.

Hundreds of thousands of people had heard the good news of salvation from sin and new life in Christ; multitudes had believed and been saved. Little boys and girls and adults of all ages and in great numbers, had been taught the Word of God. A Bible Institute had been administered, students trained and a competent Chinese staff appointed. Churches had been established and now had their own mature, spiritual Chinese pastors and elders. Men and women in jail had heard of Jesus Christ through the witness of William and Anna Englund and become new people through faith in Him. Chinese women had been taught to read and study the Scriptures. Some had become full time Bible women much used of God. Churches had been taught principles of Christian life and government, being welded together in a fellowship of love. Revival had swept again and again through all the area like a hurricane of blessing. Hidden sins had been brought to light, churches cleansed, cold hearts warmed and new fires of zeal lit for God. Englund's firm conviction that fervent, persistent prayer leads to revival had been proved times without number.

As the St. Paul climbed higher and Sian faded from view, William Englund knew that to God alone was due all honor for all had been accomplished by His Spirit. Missionaries were being forced out of Shensi, but God would remain, standing with His people amid the fierce flames of persecution until the great trumpet sound would call them home.

17

Ambassador at Large

Missionaries are often reminded of their special privilege of being an ambassador of Jesus Christ assigned to an overseas post, but they are seldom exhorted to remember that ambassadors are frequently moved around. God's servant, William Englund, was about to have a quick succession of new posts.

The St. Paul had scarcely landed when the Canton Bible Institute invited him to teach, but Canton was soon the target of a southward communist drive. The school hurriedly moved to Hong Kong taking the Englunds with them as part of the staff. He quickly settled into a familiar pattern of teaching, conferences and evangelism.

Written Chinese is the same everywhere, but spoken Cantonese is totally different from Northern Chinese. Katherine Tang, who had interpreted for Englund on his way through Hong Kong 11 years earlier, again offered her valuable assistance. On the blackboard he outlined the lesson in Chinese characters which all the class could read and understand perfectly. Then as he enlarged upon the subject in his Shensi Chinese, Katherine Tang accurately repeated the teaching in Cantonese. In this way several books of the Old Testament were surveyed so effectively that the following term Englund's teaching hours were doubled. He shared with students treasures from Job and the Psalms, all the prophetic books of the Old Testament and the Revelation.

Hong Kong island and Kowloon, a strip of Mainland China leased to the British crown colony by the Chinese government, became increasingly crowded with refugees from the Mainland. Evangelistic opportunities were unlimited. TEAM missionaries were able to rent a damp apartment as a temporary home and headquarters. They were also able to obtain permission to hold open-air services at nine public places. Oscar Beckon had succeeded in the remarkable feat of driving a Mission truck all the way from Shensi to Kowloon, and a new worker, Nils Sunwall, volunteered as driver and mechanic. Chinese Christians added their enthusiasm and an evangelistic team was ready to go. Audiences were easy to find and Englund was glad to share in preaching to thousands of spiritually hungry people.

By the time 30 TEAM missionaries had evacuated to Hong Kong it was obvious that a conference was necessary to decide on a course of action. Four days were set aside to know God's will. Englund, asked to bring a daily message, turned to the book of Ezekiel and spoke on "The hand of the Lord upon His servant." An invitation from the Field Council of TEAM missionaries in Japan to join in the work there was prayerfully considered. As in the days of the first Jerusalem council, "it seemed good to the Holy Spirit and to them" to accept, but freedom to stay was given to any who believed God had a ministry for them in Hong Kong.

The Englunds decided to stay. He still had an unfinished task at the Bible Institute and other places. He was again struggling with a problem for which he never discovered a satisfactory solution. After the majority of TEAM workers had sailed for Japan, he wrote, "we few that are left here find it difficult to meet the demands on our time that the numerous opportunities bring us." His weekly schedule included responsibility for teaching 13 books of the Bible at the Institute, regular services in British military camps, evangelism in factories and prisons, chapel services, visits to villages, and a Sunday school on the roof of their apartment building. When attendance reached 80 the children were asked to meet in the Bible Institute. Anna Englund shared with other TEAM women in housekeeping duties, village work and English classes. Special services in all parts of Hong Kong and Kowloon "kept our brethren in charge of the public address system very busy," reported Englund. Thousands heard of Christ through messages in song, pictures and word, and hundreds turned to Christ. The Lord had not brought His servants to South China in vain. Harvest had come.

News seeping through from the Mainland was alternately encouraging and gloomy. The Sian Bible Institute had begun a new term with 60 students. The Sian church used a large tent for two campaigns in which there were 300 public decisions for Christ, and in the chapels a continuous stream of weary, burdened people had found rest and forgiveness in the Savior . . . but by mid 1949 news of another kind came. Shanghai, Sian and Canton had all fallen before Mao Tse-tung's relentless drive for power. Chiang Kai-shek's government had moved back to its World War II capital of Chungking. Standing on the flat roof of his Hong Kong apartment and looking north toward the hills, Englund recalled Isaiah's reference to "the burden of the valley of vision." Thinking of China in a dark valley of trouble and perplexity, he remembered that in such dismal places God had often given new visions of Himself. The uppermost question in Englund's heart was whether doors so wonderfully opened for preaching the gospel were to be closed forever, and hundreds of millions of people doomed to the tyranny of atheistic philosophy. Pressed down by the gigantic problem, he began to pray, his eyes open to the heavens. Over one of the distant peaks hovered a threatening thunder cloud, black and menacing, but suddenly, in its very center, what appeared to be a square door opened as if in assurance that the Lord is always able to open doors which no man can shut.

The Englunds waited in vain, however, for an all clear signal to return to Shensi. Scraps of news continued to be alternately good and bad. Pastor Tuan wrote that the fall term of the Bible Institute opened with 50 students, but a few months later Englund learned with deep sorrow that this faithful and gifted servant of the Lord had been accidentally knocked down and killed by a military truck. As he wrestled with the problem of why God had allowed the death of one whom the churches needed so much, Englund found assurance in the words of Nahum that "the Lord hath His way in the whirlwind and in the storm and the clouds are the dust of His feet." He wrote home, "We may question why the enemy has been permitted to sweep over the whole land like a fierce whirlwind, raising the dust, disturbing missionary work and putting things under a dark cloud of uncertainty, but looking higher we see how the Lord's way is above the clouds, and that there is no need on His part to wait until the dust settles in order to get a clear view. Both clouds and dust are already under His feet as He moves forward to final victory." The same letter with the sad news of Pastor Tuan's death also told of continuing evangelism and many decisions for Christ. The Spirit of God could not be stopped but was moving like an irresistible wind over the land.

Constantly urging others to persist in fervent prayer for China, Englund himself never gave up his exhausting battles with the powers of darkness. In mind, heart and prayer he traveled the well-known roads to Lantien, Hsingping, Kienhsien, Pingliang and other towns and villages around Sian. Names of many a pastor, elder, and countless church members were brought before the Lord, always with pleadings that God would show mercy to thousands of others. Many Christians, like Peter, were being sifted as wheat, and prayer was needed that their faith should not fail. Subtle means were being used to entice Christians away from the truth, but a good foundation had been laid with Jesus Christ Himself as the cornerstone.

Churches which had remained stedfast through the crises of famine, disease, drought and war refused to deny their Lord. A special request from Pastor Wang Shih-kuang was a constant call to prayer. "First of all," he had written, "we ask you to pray for us that through the infilling of the Holy Spirit we may be able to stand fast in the midst of the present perilous times, and kept waiting for the Lord's return. Please pray for the church and for your fellow workers here that there may be an increasing fullness of spiritual power for revival and for the Lord's work." *That urgent request has never been canceled. To ignore it would be sin.*

Englund wrote letter after letter calling for prayer for China in her hour of desperate need. The Scriptures were his greatest encouragement. Referring to Rev. 7:14, *these are they who have come out of the great tribulation,* he reasoned that if God the Almighty "will make the outcome of the greatest suffering so wondrous, then we can fully trust Him to perform wonders in and through the trials, dangers, frustrations and perplexities of our present day." Within a few weeks, he received news from Lantien that 127 new believers had recently been baptized.

As The Evangelical Alliance Mission looked for new ways of ministering to the great Chinese nation, Englund was also seeking fresh guidance. There were two reasons for remaining in Hong Kong. The Evangelical Free Church had urged him to continue teaching in their Bible Institute . . . and secondly, William and Anna Englund disliked the idea of moving out from a last corner of China which "after so many years of missionary work . . . had become part of their very being." On the other hand, the American Consul, believing that all China was about to fall to communism, and uncertain of repercussions in Hong Kong, had advised all U.S. citizens to leave. Also, Anna's health was not good. High blood pressure which troubled her in Shensi had recurred in Hong Kong and put her in the hospital for two weeks. After further physical weakness, she was advised by doctors to leave Hong Kong.

At the Chinese New Year, amid the thunder of firecrackers so loud that even his deaf ears registered some noise, Englund set aside a special time of prayer to seek to know God's will. His decision was to apply for permission to enter Japan, which was then under Allied control, and at the same time make a reservation on a ship sailing for the United States a few months later. When weeks passed without the permits arriving, the Englunds were again uncertain about their next move. In answer to further prayer, God, in that mysterious way which all who have close dealings with Him fully understand, made known His will. Passages to America were canceled. A few days later permits to enter Japan were received from Allied headquarters, Tokyo.

For nearly half a century Englund had given himself wholeheartedly to service in China and almost to the last day continued teaching the Bible as energetically as ever. He gave up classes at the Bible Institute, but regularly brought devotional messages and spoke at their special days of prayer. He continued with private classes on the book of Revelation and accepted invitations from Chinese and English-speaking churches. His final engagement in Kowloon, physically but not politically part of the China Mainland, was a conference for Christian workers and students, at which he spoke six times. In spare moments he helped Anna to pack. Farewell gatherings arranged by the Free Church, the Bible Institute, and fellow missionaries overwhelmed them. When sailing day arrived they were exhausted mentally and physically. God knew and had a surprise in store. Ahead of them were 18 days of pleasant cruising.

The Englunds stood on the deck of the big Dutch Royal Interocean Line freighter MV Tegelberg. Moorings were cast off and as the ship eased away from the dock, friends old and new waved farewell. The Tegelberg glided cautiously through the crowded waters of Hong Kong harbor, alive with sampans, scurrying launches, placid junks, naval vessels and ocean liners . . . but Englund's eyes were on the coastline of "dear old China" slowly receding in the haze. He turned towards Anna, his eyes dimmed by tears. He could not speak. The land they loved would never be forgotten; they were leaving home.

When he had booked passages on the Tegelberg, Englund had not known that the route was via the Philippines. Thankful for the urgently needed rest, they sailed south to Manila where Englund had the unexpected pleasure of seeing his sister-in-law, principal of the Mapa High School, waiting to welcome them at the dock. Two weeks later the islands of Japan appeared on the horizon, and after calling at several ports, the Tegelberg tied up at Yokohama. God's ambassador, William Englund, stepped ashore ready for a new assignment.

18

Mission Accomplished

Strong emotions and vivid memories inevitably flooded the hearts and minds of most China missionaries on arrival in Japan after enduring the agonies of the long war in Asia. Only unquestioning obedience to God's command and the constraining love of Christ had taken them there. For the Englunds it was an extra encouragement to see six of their China comrades standing on the Yokohama pier to welcome them. All were fellow missionaries in Shensi who had come to make them feel at home. Even better things were to follow. They had hardly settled into a cozy little apartment in Tokyo when Englund was writing to friends, "we have already taken part in some meetings and had the joy of seeing souls decide for Christ."

All his life Englund preached with a keen sense of urgency. *Like Luther, he lived as if Christ had died yesterday, were risen today, and coming tomorrow.* His determination that the greatest number of people in Northwest China should hear the gospel in the shortest possible time by the best possible means had resulted, through the Holy Spirit's mighty working, in strong churches reliant on God alone. In Japan Englund felt the same urgency and had the same aim. In a land whose Emperor had publicly repudiated his claim to divinity, and whose gods had been discredited, Englund quickly realized that the Devil and other powers of darkness which had so long ruled Japan would work feverishly to fill the spiritual emptiness with false new doctrines and weird cults. Some of them were doubly dangerous, having a smattering of Christian truth mixed with a mass of lies. The angel's command to the women at the empty tomb of Christ came as God's voice to Englund, "Go quickly and tell." On the first Easter morning Christ's enemies concocted a lie and sped it on its way with bribes. Truth followed in hot pursuit. Japan also needed to hear quickly, before strange new gods deceived her afresh, or fictitious old gods were resurrected.

Some of the former Shensi missionaries, picturesquely known as "old China hands," were making brave efforts to learn Japanese. Englund could not. No sound penetrated his deaf ears. He had, however, the advantage of being a good writer of Chinese. A peculiar quirk in Japanese history helped him.

Centuries earlier the Japanese had developed a passion for Chinese culture. They already had two forms of phonetic script which were quite adequate for writing all words in the language, but their preference was for the more elegant style of Chinese writing. Although Chinese and Japanese are entirely different and have nothing in common grammatically, the Japanese made the astonishing decision to write their language in Chinese characters but to continue their own pronunciation. It was rather as if an American should write words such as *table* and *chair* in Chinese characters but continue to pronounce them as before. It was part of the Japanese philosophy that appearance is more important than content. The modern climax of this unusual decision is that Japanese writing is a complicated mixture of Chinese and Japanese, liberally sprinkled with English.

Englund was happy to find that he could read and understand all Japanese words written in Chinese style (even though he pronounced them the Chinese way), and that Japanese could read and understand much of what he wrote in Chinese (even though they pronounced the words in the Japanese way). They could write to each other, but not talk.

Englund's ministry in Japan, however, began with a gospel message to Chinese in a Yokosuka prison. His Northern dialect was understood perfectly. Later the same day he preached at a beach service when two U.S. sailors were baptized. In the evening he spoke for the first time to a Japanese congregation with the help of an interpreter.

Many times in China God had blessed Englund's prayerful ministry and faithful preaching with revival. His prayer that in Japan "the Word of the Lord may speed and triumph" was answered in the same way. More than 120 TEAM missionaries met for their annual conference in the beautiful mountain resort of Karuizawa. A week had been set aside for discussions on policy and strategy. The majority of the workers were young and inexperienced. Problems of language study, oriental culture, heathen religions and effective evangelism were enormous. Financial difficulties, housing needs, and lack of church buildings added to the dilemma. Questions were debated, matters tabled, and ideas discussed but solutions not found. By the end of the week little had been decided, except that the conference should be extended. Englund, asked to speak the next morning, gave a message on "Opened eyes and burning hearts" from Luke's account of Christ meeting with discouraged disciples on the Emmaus road. In the prayer time that followed, the conference was shaken as with a wind from heaven. Tears and confession, prayer and praise continued throughout the day. With revival having come, problems went. When business sessions were resumed, mountains of difficulty had become molehills as God by His Spirit led His people to His solutions.

Not surprisingly, Englund was assigned to teach in Bible school. He found in Pastor Sukigara a fellow worker and excellent interpreter from English to Japanese. "Sukigara" means "hoe handle," and Englund laughingly suggested that he should sow, and the Pastor do the hoeing. In the classroom he wrote the lesson outline on the blackboard in Chinese which his students could understand and copy. The practice sometimes carried him back to the old days and he unconsciously reverted to speaking in Chinese. A warm friendship developed between Englund and Pastor Sukigara and many were brought to Christ through their united ministry in evangelism. When Anna Englund contracted a serious infection on her face, it was Pastor Sukigara who called Japanese Christians together for special prayer and the Lord speedily answered.

Englund's responsibilities were three classes and one chapel service a week in the Bible school. He was also active in evangelistic campaigns in new churches and Gospel Halls, and in Bible teaching at conferences. Prayer, however, remained his first priority. A letter written early in 1952 began, "We will give ourselves to prayer and the ministry of the Word." He added, "The Lord has led us to give more time to prayer these past months. The needs and possibilities, opportunities and obstacles, God's workings and enemy activities, the power of the gospel and the strongholds of darkness, open doors and sin-locked hearts, all these conflicting conditions and influences are encountered and experienced in the rescue work of souls in this land these days, and most urgently call for prayer that there may be victory through the power of the Holy Spirit. The Lord truly is pushing His work forward through opened doors, but to bring souls from darkness to light, and from the power of Satan to God is no easy matter in a land where the prince of darkness is so strongly entrenched. Spiritually, people are in complete bondage in spite of intellectual attainments and a pleasing politeness. A soul-stirring revival in and through the churches is urgently needed. This is our prayer burden and apart from other things, there is the daily pressure upon us of our anxiety for all the churches in our China field. Conditions are growing more perilous to our dear fellow workers and Christians there. The only way of reaching them is via the Throne of Grace. No iron curtain can close that way of communication."

The Englunds' final months in Japan were a time of continuous blessing from the Lord and happy fellowship with His servants. On March 17, 1952 a group of TEAM missionaries, including several "old China hands," together with Japanese Christians and a U.S. Army chaplain and friends, crowded into the Mission headquarters in Tokyo. It was William Englund's 70th birthday. Rev. Julius Bergstrom, born in Shensi of pioneer missionary parents, was in charge of the celebration. Chaplain Emanuel Carlsen gave the main address, and others provided music, made speeches, and asked God's continued blessing on His faithful servant. In no way could the music reach him, but all other parts of the program had been typed out for his enjoyment. His feelings were best expressed in a letter to his "dear Supporters and Prayer-helpers." He wrote, "To God goes all the praise and glory for His unfailing grace throughout my three score and ten years. In the meeting the night before (the birthday celebration) we had the joy of seeing several souls accept Christ as Savior. I could not have wished for a better ending of my old year. We trust the Lord to continually direct our paths in His blessed service."

A few months later, the Englunds went aboard the freighter Pacific Transport expecting to reach San Francisco within two weeks, but three days later the ship was drifting helplessly in heavy fog 1,000 miles out to sea without its rudder. An approaching typhoon added to the peril of the crippled freighter. The foghorn never ceased its mournful warning and S.O.S. calls went out continually.

Christians aboard ship also sent out distress signals to "the God of heaven, which hath made the sea and the dry land." And the Lord who rebuked wind and waves on the Sea of Galilee dissipated the threatening typhoon, and brought the freighter Seaborns to the rescue. Guided by radar, it came alongside at midnight. In rain, fog and darkness, the passengers were lowered in a lifeboat and transferred to the Seaborne which then towed the rudderless ship back to Yokohama. The Englunds "felt that the Lord must have had a purpose also in this," and bowed to God's superior wisdom, when through the delay they regretably missed their daughter Winifred's graduation.

A few days later they again sailed out of Yokohama and each day had the opportunity of teaching the Scriptures aboard ship all the way to Los Angeles. When they walked down the gangplank, their daughter Grace rushed to meet them with open arms. It was the beginning of two years of furlough full of sunshine and shadows.

Anna's father, 96 years old, passed peacefully into the presence of Christ before she could reach Jersey City, but in August, 1952, their joy was full when Winifred married Charles Christensen. In Japan Englund had met three people who had known the bridegroom at three stages of his life, and from their reports, had been well satisfied with his daughter's choice of a husband. With his usual modesty, Englund wrote that "the bride's father performed the marriage." Actually he did more than that. As a smiling father, looking smart in a dark blue suit, he led Winifred down the aisle of Judson Baptist Church and gave her away. He then assumed the role of pastor and conducted the rest of the service. Through all the perils of travel, sickness, war, banditry, bombing, internment, and long sea voyages, God had marvelously preserved the family and brought them to another highlight of happiness.

The following month Salem Church, Chicago, overwhelmed them with a double-header by combining celebrations for their homecoming and silver wedding anniversary. The same church was the scene of another happy experience. Isabella Wong and Dr. Paul Chan of Hong Kong, who affectionately regarded the Englunds as if they were their own parents, had delayed their wedding so that Rev. Englund could conduct the service. They were the first Chinese couple to be married in Salem Church. The following day a shadow fell as Anna Englund entered the hospital for major surgery. To the comfort of God's presence and the ministry of angels was added the blessing of having her own daughter as nurse.

Before furlough ended, one of Englund's dreams came true. He visited Teien, Minnesota, where 55 years earlier he had preached his first sermon. Taking as the text "Looking unto Jesus as He walked, he saith, 'Behold the Lamb of God'," he emphasized that because John's own eyes were on Jesus, he was able to point others to Him. "It reminds us of how looking unto Jesus and pointing others to Him have, by the grace of God, been our chief occupation throughout the years that have passed," he wrote after seeing Teien again.

There were other blessings during the brief time in Minnesota. After traveling on a train which Englund described as "speedless and foodless," he met old friends in his boyhood town of St. Hilaire. Some had been in a Sunday school class he had taught 50 years earlier. He also saw again the farm house built by his father and shed tears as he stood in his mother's outdoor place of prayer. During her earthly life she never knew how marvelously God would answer prayer for her son William. His final stop in Minnesota was Thief River Falls where he had been converted during a revival 60 years earlier. On that great day he never guessed that revival through the Holy Spirit would be the hallmark of his own long ministry.

Shadows continued to come and go. A telephone call brought the sad news that their daughter Winifred's first child had lived only a few days. "She was a tiny bud that the Lord wanted for His heavenly garden," explained Englund. Their skies were again clouded when Anna needed major surgery once more, but in answer to prayer, God granted an excellent recovery. Sunshine burst upon the family when their daughter Miriam and her husband arrived on leave from his work in Arabia . . . and sunshine and shadow were about equal in a predicament which Englund described with help from the Scriptures. "Solomon, the wise preacher, says, 'The grinders cease because they are so few,' "but in my case there is now none left, so this past month not only has grinding ceased but I have also felt it difficult to speak. I am now waiting for the dentist to replace what he earlier found it necessary to extract," he confided.

"Come over and help us . . . immediately we endeavored to go . . . gathering that the Lord had called us for to preach the gospel unto them." Englund was about to resume his ministry among the Chinese. More than 70 years old, he was not interested in retirement or in becoming a furloughed missionary. His feet were quick to follow his heart, inseparably one with the Chinese people. Days of prayer and fasting led to fixing a time limit for knowing the will of God. Four days before the deadline, he received a letter from Dr. David Johnson, General Director of TEAM, then on a visit to Taiwan, suggesting that there was work there for him to do. He gladly obeyed without delay. In Salem Free Church, Chicago, which had so long supported them by prayer and gifts, William and Anna Englund were commissioned anew for service overseas.

19

Unwavering

For the seventh time Englund was ready to take the gospel to the Chinese, faithfully fulfilling God's command given him more than half a century earlier. Parting from family and friends had not become any easier and it was a painful experience he always dreaded, but his tender heart found comfort in a stockpile of happy memories. Furlough had been full of blessings and now, for the first time, the Englunds were sailing from New York, traveling to Taiwan via Europe. Englund added to his global ministry by preaching at a Sunday service on the SS United States as she crossed the Atlantic.

Special meetings had also been arranged for him in Norway and Sweden. After the brief interlude of an "upsetting experience on the North Sea," he was in Norway again after many years. Still fluent in the language, he had no difficulty in preaching. His wife was also delighted to find that she had no great problem with Norwegian. God's blessing was abundant, as it was in China, and when Englund reached Oslo, to be welcomed by relatives, fellow workers and friends, his heart was overflowing with praise.

An unexpected and violent attack of eczema on his face limited his visit and shortened the time in Sweden, where other China comrades were eagerly looking for him. Swedish, the language of his boyhood, had remained his preference in private prayer and was put to use once more in preaching. With a short stop in Denmark to minister there, Englund and his wife returned to Southampton to embark on the SS Canton, destination Hong Kong. He immediately arranged for a daily meeting in his cabin and evening classes in Ephesians in the Tourist Class nursery. The one sad note on the pleasant month's voyage was a radiogram advising that a little grandson had lived only a few days.

Hong Kong was glad to see the Englunds again, and friends of the Free Church were ready with an enthusiastic welcome as the Canton tied up. A full schedule of preaching engagements had been arranged. He was not ashore long before he was speaking at a united missionary prayer meeting and then at a Chinese service. Hong Kong Keswick invited him to share in a convention at the Tai Po Orphanage on a beautiful hill overlooking the sea. The other speaker was Dr. McCoy, a retired American minister, who enjoyed introducing himself as "the real McCoy." Englund, already 72, wrote that Dr. McCoy "is several years my senior, yet the Lord has sent him out to foreign fields in his old age, and is using him mightily in blessed proof of what His grace and power are able to do." God knew Englund needed such encouragement. Ahead was much hard physical work, a heavy schedule and the tension of living in the shadow of war.

In October, 1954, William and Anna arrived in Taiwan with the Word of the Lord ringing in their ears, "Let them give glory unto the Lord and declare His praise in the islands." Fellow workers, Chinese friends and courteous customs officers reduced baggage problems to a minimum, but finding a place to live was not so easy. For several weeks the Englunds lived in what he described as "a chaotic mess." In Taiwan, TEAM was following methods well tried in North China. Pioneer evangelism was quickly followed by training courses for new believers so that under God strong churches could be established with Chinese leadership. A Bible school was vital to the plan. Undeterred by threats of war from communist armies massed across the narrow Taiwan Straits, veteran missionary Fred Nelson had bought an old country house as the first unit of a Bible school. With financial help from one or two home churches, simple additions had been made. Eager, talented, young Christians were easier to find than buildings, money and teachers. William Englund was more than welcome.

The best accommodation available was a three and one half room brick-floored apartment. With his energy and her resourcefulness, the Englunds began making a home for themselves. They needed no reminder that they were pilgrims on the earth. They had been making homes and moving all their lives, but Englund found that the task took a little longer than before. As always, he never refused any invitation to share in an evangelistic effort, but felt the handicap of Taiwan's hot and humid climate. Threescore years and ten also slowed down his nimble efforts and in letters he succumbed to identifying with old folks . . . but he was ready to teach.

A class of new students had been accepted in the Bible School, doubling the number of class hours, and putting such a load on Englund that he was not able to get away for special meetings. He somehow managed to squeeze in time for correspondence, writing two equally long letters of thanks, one for a gift of $2, and the other for a contribution of $1,000 for the work.

Englund was convinced that knowing and spreading the Word of God always results in additional believers. In proof, he would quote Acts 6:7, "The word of God increased and the number of disciples multiplied." For this reason he never deviated from concentrating on prayer and teaching the Scriptures. In his first term in the Bible School he taught ten books synthetically and others analytically, but that was only part of his activity. Knowing had to be followed by spreading, so Englund led his students in practical evangelism. On weekends there were meetings in homes and in the streets. Sunday schools were started in villages, and on Christmas Sunday, 1954, over 300 excited and happy children met in a large tent for a special program.

The majority of Chinese in Taiwan followed the old calendar for the New Year. Stores were closed and business came to a stop. Streets were filled with crowds on their way to the temples, noisily encouraged by exploding firecrackers. Feasts and family gatherings added to the gaiety. To Englund it was a marvelous opportunity for evangelism. Following the pattern of the old Sian Bible Institute, teachers and students from the Taiwan Bible School moved out among the crowds with the same compassion that Jesus had shown for people. Lessons learned in the classroom were put into action and results followed. God added to His church. In a Taichung church, for example, Englund was especially thrilled to see an old couple together with two younger members of their family come forward to be counseled after an evening service.

God's blessing on the Bible School created a problem. Students were between 20 and 30 years old, some from the China Mainland and others born in Taiwan. A number were married, one with a wife and child on the Mainland whom he had not seen for eight years. Many had been converted after fleeing to Taiwan, but as they came to know Christ better, their radiant testimonies attracted others to the school. The dilemma facing TEAM missionaries at their annual conference was that more students were applying to Bible School than they could accommodate. It was a problem no one had anticipated. Prayer followed prayer until the distance between heaven and earth narrowed and Jesus Himself stood in the midst. God also spoke through His Word as Englund shared such promises from Isaiah as, "Fear not, I will help thee," and without knowing where funds, extra teachers and accommodations would come from, the conference decided in faith to accept a freshman class of eight students.

Even the weather that year was an encouragement to trust God. Spring had been exceptionally dry and rice fields were hard and cracked. Newspapers predicted the worst drought in 60 years. A shutdown of hydroelectric power stations for an hour or more daily warned that disaster threatened. With memories of how God had wonderfully answered prayer for rain in his early days in Shensi, Englund joined hundreds of other Christians in calling on the Lord to end the drought. The answer came in mighty showers which quenched the thirsty fields, turned turbines back to full power and transformed Taiwan into a fresh, green island. Soon rice seedlings were sending up tender shoots in little fields around the Bible School, ready to be transplanted. As Englund watched busy farmers and their families in their backbreaking work, he thought of the Scriptures and of the school. "The seed is the Word of God," and also, "the good seed are the children of the kingdom." "In the Lord's field both Word and lives must be sown," he wrote, comparing the Bible School to a rice patch ready for transplanting. The work had, in fact, already started. Sunday classes for children had developed into regular preaching services and youth work in six large villages, with Bible School students taking full responsibility. Miracles were taking place. In one village a man was delivered from despair so deep that he had contemplated suicide. Filled with the joy of salvation, he gave his house as a place of worship.

Blessings on Taiwan did not eclipse the suffering of countless Christians on the Mainland. Constant bombardment of two small Nationalist-held islands only a mile from the Mainland coast was a thundering reminder that war was still being fought. President Chiang Kai-shek and his wife both spoke over the radio on Easter Sunday, 1955 witnessing to their faith in Christ, and they had previously set aside Good Friday as a day of prayer and fasting for churches behind the Bamboo Curtain. In the broadcast, Madame Chiang referred clearly to redemption through faith in the risen Christ. The messages were printed in all Taiwan newspapers.

By June, 1955, the Bible School had completed two wonderful years and Englund ended his first full year as teacher. Problems, trials and the tension of war had been overcome by prayer and thanksgiving so that the school closed for a summer vacation with joyful praise to God. The occasion was also a farewell to Mr. Nelson, who was leaving for furlough. In thanking him for starting the school, one of the students caused laughter by his humor, but when he seized a piano-accordian to play "God be with you till we meet again," he burst into tears before completing the first stanza.

By the fall, the School was ready for 12 new students, four of them women. The problems of staff and accommodations had been solved by assigning the senior class to full time practical work in various churches, and requiring them to give monthly reports on their work. A well-known Chinese pastor, invited to speak at the opening of the new term, failed to arrive and, in Englund's modest words, "Thus it suddenly fell on someone else to give the message, and God gave the blessing." He did not say what text he chose. They met in the enlarged and renovated chapel, but a compound for women students remained an urgent need.

Englund's share of teaching was formidable. Long before the 6:00 A.M. morning devotions with students, he was up for his own time of Bible study and prayer. He taught the entire New Testament synthetically and the books of Daniel and Romans analytically. Thorough preparation for classwork took long hours and drained his energy. His notes for lecturing or preaching were always written in Chinese. He regularly took turns speaking in chapel and on Sundays went with students to preach in the villages.

Total deafness had become a normal part of his life. The only voice ever heard was that of God Himself. Occasionally the harsh reality of his handicap impinged itself on him. Winifred, who began her evangelistic career with the one-sentence Chinese sermon in Shensi, was now broadcasting regularly over a Christian station in Chicago. Copies of the tapes were mailed to Taiwan for her mother to hear, but William Englund, denied the special pleasure of hearing his daughter's voice, had to be satisfied with a typed copy of the script. On the other hand, he was immune to sounds of war. Other teachers had to compete with the chattering of machine guns, the sharp crack of rifles and the thud of mortars as Nationalist troops in realistic war maneuvers prepared for a battle to recover their Mainland. Englund rested quietly in a promise given at the beginning of the school year, "then came Jesus and stood in the midst and said, 'Peace be unto you'."

At the Easter conference in 1956 strong chords of victory echoed like jubilant musical bells. Missionary children on vacation from Taichung Morrison Academy were able to attend with their parents, adding joy and liveliness to the occasion. Englund wrote that the Lord "again used the oldest of our Formosa TEAMers in giving daily devotional Bible talks, this time leading us into what he called 'Resurrection Retreats with Christ.' God's blessing and the Spirit's stirring melted, unified and refreshed all who heard."

As Englund prayed for more Bible School teachers, and additional accommodations for students, he wistfully remembered how easily Elisha had solved a similar problem by going to the forest with his students and cutting down all the trees needed for lumber. He was thankful that God who miraculously raised an iron ax head from a river bed could raise funds for buildings. In fact, help was closer than he knew. Nearby was a river with plenty of large stones. Rev. Oscar Beckon, with better equipment than Elisha ever dreamed of, arrived with a truck and took students to the river for loads of stones to use in a foundation for a women's dormitory. Staff needs were met by the arrival of a missionary couple, and God answered prayer by healing and bringing back three students who had a TB infection.

By the end of 1956 the Bible School was in full swing with a total enrollment of 40 students. When representatives of 14 new churches

131

God established through TEAM met at the School for a conference, they were delighted by what they saw. And Dr. Vernon Mortenson, then Assistant General Director of the Mission and former Shensi worker, on a visit to Taiwan also saw much cause for praise. Students had to live in cramped quarters, but the presence of the Lord eliminated friction and created a happy fellowship.

On Sundays many villagers attended services in the School chapel. As the majority were people speaking a local dialect, Englund had his messages interpreted into Taiwanese. None of the power was lost in the process. Interest and attendance increased and, during the first four months of a new school year, nearly 50 people of all ages had accepted Christ as Savior.

As Christmas drew near, Englund, like most missionaries, became painfully aware of being far from home. As so often, a parallel situation in Scripture was his comfort. "As we on the far-away field longingly think of our dear ones and friends at home, it is a comfort to note how all those in the Christmas story—Mary and Joseph, shepherds and magi, angels and Jesus—were away from home, too. We thank God for His unspeakable gift and for the privilege of being used by Him both in sending and being sent," he wrote in a prayer letter.

When the first term closed at the end of January, Englund felt a strange weariness. It was not physical. He was still able to do his daily exercises with military precision. He was certainly not spiritually exhausted, but continued to go from strength to strength, praising God. But he had what he described as a "head-weariness." Then like a little child at the end of a long day, he turned to his Father asking what was to be done. William Englund had always found that guidance comes through much prayer and God speaking through the Scriptures. This time was no exception. A whole day was given to prayer and listening for God's clear voice. Then he was ready, his inner hearing sharpened by hours of closest communion with Christ. Englund picked up his Bible. "Return unto thine own house and show how great things God hath done unto thee," he read, and looking again, his eyes fell on the words, "Rise, let us be going." The time had come for William Gideon Englund to retire. "But not yet from active service," he hurriedly added when he wrote to tell friends of the decision.

He celebrated his 75th birthday quietly in Taiwan. Still quite busy, he had little time for strictly personal matters. As well as helping on occasion at the Bible school, he had opportunities to preach, and continually "thanked the Lord for grace and strength given His old servant in meetings here and there, and for blessings of spiritual refreshing and the salvation of souls." He visited the Taichung jail with Oscar Beckon and saw God so move the hearts of the prisoners that 40 accepted Christ as Savior. The final days in Taiwan passed like swift waters of a rushing stream. In June he happily watched the first Bible School graduation and later the same month the Englunds attended their last TEAM conference on Chinese soil.

Painful farewells were said on July 2, 1957, but on this occasion no ocean liner reluctantly inched away from a dock to extend the agony. For the first time Englund and his wife were flying home. The route took them via Hong Kong where old friends met to bid them Godspeed. Soon their plane was climbing steeply from the rocky island and heading east. Englund looked out of the window. To the north he could see the hazy outline of the China Mainland. Not a single person was visible from such a height, but there were millions of them, millions and millions, who were struggling, sweating, suffering and dying. Much farther than the eye could see were the Yangtze and Yellow Rivers like giant veins reaching to the heartland of the country. But Englund's thoughts went still farther to where he had prayed and preached and seen God work miracles.

Churches born in travail, nurtured in suffering and matured in pain were enduring new trials in Shensi province. A cloud bank suddenly blocked the view. Perhaps he was glimpsing his beloved China for the last time, but as long as he lived nothing would ever separate its people from his prayers. "For what is our hope, or joy, or crown of rejoicing? Are not even ye in the presence of our Lord Jesus Christ at His coming?," Paul had written to Christians in Thessalonica. The Englund's feelings towards China were exactly the same.

20

Doctor of Letters

The Englund's prayer letters from 1958 on give the impression that they were still working either in Sian or Taiwan. The address, however, was usually Chicago. In thought, heart and spirit they had never left the Mainland. By prayer Englund was still an active member of the Taiwan Bible School staff. Letters from the principal, Mr. Su Liang-i, one of his dearest friends, kept him informed of progress and problems, and he rejoiced to hear that Su's gifts and calling were recognized by ordination. In daily wrestlings with the powers of darkness, Englund continued to fight a battle begun more than half a century earlier in Shensi. Conflicting rumors and a trickle of news brought little comfort. He wept on learning that three Chinese pastors to whom he was bound in love and service had been brutally murdered and that others had been thrown in jail. Enemies of Christ were on a rampage and Shensi soil was red with the blood of faithful men who "loved not their lives unto death."

Over the years Englund had developed considerable skill in expressing himself clearly and forcefully in prayer letters which invariably centered around a particular spiritual truth, and were often lightened with his sparkling humor. His literary ability was inherited and developed by his daughter Winifred. How Englund found time to write regularly throughout his busy missionary career is a mystery, but correspondence with prayer partners never failed. Anna Englund's share in this ministry was considerable. With so-called retirement, Englund had an opportunity to fulfill a request from Chinese Christians and fellow missionaries in Taiwan that his lectures and sermons be published. The task kept him busy for ten years, molding the pattern of his daily schedule. Insulated against all distracting noise by deafness he closed the door of his bedroom study to be alone with God. In a silence unbroken even by the rustling leaves of his Chinese Bible, he turned to familiar passages. Ears open to God's Spirit, he wrote in Chinese, stopping occasionally to consult his dictionary. As he looked over old notes, his mind went back to days when God's blessing fell like torrential Shensi rain, or when the burning presence of God's Spirit was like the fierce heat of summer. In his little room, surrounded by Chinese scrolls, texts, pictures and furniture, it seemed as though he was in Sian preparing for special meetings in Lantien.

With praise for what God had done, Englund turned from happy memories to the work at hand. His commentary on Genesis was nearly finished. "In chapter 46 verse 1 we find Jacob at Beersheba," he wrote. "God met him with a fresh vision. We have here three 'I wills" — 'I will make thee a great nation . . . I will go down with thee into Egypt . . . I will also bring thee up again.' Oftentimes the Lord is more ready with His 'I will' than we are with our 'I will'." As Englund wrote, the China Sunday School Union in Taiwan was waiting impatiently to print and publish the first volume of the commentary. When he laid down his pen for the last time, Englund's legacy to the Chinese church was a scholarly and spiritual exposition of the first eight books of the Old Testament. His work on I Samuel was incomplete when the Lord called him to higher service.

Englund never had the slightest intention of giving up active service when he and his wife finished their ministry in Taiwan, but he never expected to undertake a world tour at the age of 82. It began with an invitation from their daughter, Miriam Lindgren, and her husband to spend a couple of weeks with them in Saudi Arabia where they were stationed with the Arabian American Oil Company. Dr. Vernon Mortenson, a former China co-worker and now General Director of TEAM, enthusiastically supported the idea and suggested that their itinerary should include European countries where the Mission's work was relatively new. Salem Evangelical Free Church, which had so long supported them, added their encouragement. Careful comparison of fares showed that it would be cheaper to fly around the world than to make a round trip from Chicago to Saudi Arabia.

What had been contemplated as a family reunion gradually developed into a global tour with the primary object of strengthening the hands of TEAM missionaries and sharing blessings with them. A seasoned, scarred old warrior, victorious in the power of the Lord in many a battle was going to visit young soldiers, some on the firing line for the first time, to cheer them on.

William once more went through the familiar routine of packing his bag. All other travel details were of necessity left to Anna. Whenever he watched his wife lining up for reservations, tickets or to make inquiries, Englund felt the heavy handicap of his deafness. But God watched too, never overlooking Anna's labor of love which made her husband's ministry possible and effective all throughout their married life.

A magnificent sendoff by the Salem church resembled yet another commissioning service. For the eighth time they were on their way as ambassadors of Jesus Christ. Their triumphant tour was like a stretched version of a chapter from the Acts of the Apostles. A reunion with relatives and friends in Norway was a happy beginning; then two days in London, England, renewing old friendships at the China Inland Mission headquarters were followed by a stop in Paris where Englund preached to a group of French Christians and their friends, and rejoiced to see one accept Christ. TEAM missionaries in Portugal, struggling with every kind of difficulty, were the next to be refreshed and encouraged by a visit from the Englunds. They continued on to Madrid where the spirit of fiercely charging bulls seemed to have pervaded the driver of every car speeding along narrow streets. In the gay, restless and religious city, God was bringing a pure church into existence. Englund's fellow missionaries were more inspired with a message he shared with them than he was by a very long Spanish service arranged by the Protestant church of Madrid. He did not hear a word, and would not have understood if he had. Supper at 10:30 P.M. was a Spanish custom for which he was not prepared and it was a very weary William Englund who thankfully sank into a comfortable bed at the end of a long day.

Although TEAM has no work in Italy, the Englunds visited Rome on the suggestion of a friend in their home church. Not in the pomp and glitter of magnificent buildings did they feel most at home, but in the catacombs where persecuted Christians had once found refuge and a place of prayer. In Greece, Englund's eyes shone with all the excitement of a small boy as he nimbly climbed Mars Hill and stood where Paul had stood. Pointing at the marble Parthenon, brilliant white in the sunshine, Englund exclaimed, "God dwells not in temples made with hands."

Israel was next on their route, and for eight happy days William and Anna walked where Jesus had walked, and saw what He had seen. Years of Bible teaching could not have been better preparation for visiting the land of Abraham, Isaac and Jacob, seeing the scenes of Saul's and David's exploits, and walking the narrow streets of Jerusalem, Bethlehem and Bethany. Vivid explanations by their Christian guide, Elias, were hurriedly scribbled down by Anna so that William could understand what he was seeing. Listening, and writing, she did not find it easy to be ears for two people.

It was Thursday evening. Across the Kidron Valley the golden dome of the Mosque of Omar gleamed in the moonlight. Jerusalem was silent and unlit. No glow came from the temple area where callous men on a Passover night had once struck a bargain with the betrayer of God's Son. But the olive trees, sturdy with old age, were still there in the Garden of Gethsemane, and beneath one of them sat William and Anna Englund, and Elias. It was no time for talking. Their thoughts were on another Thursday night, long centuries before, when beneath the dark shadow of those same trees, Jesus had lain prostrate in an agony no man will ever understand. Within a few hours He was hanging from a bloody cross on Golgotha, dying for our sins. "Behold the Lamb of God which taketh away the sin of the world" — that had been the text of Englund's first sermon, and the basis of all he had preached since. It was the only ground of his own assurance of salvation . . . and suddenly the silence of Gethsemane was broken with sounds of praise as William Englund, tears streaming down his face, poured out thanksgiving to God for all His grace and love.

By October, 1964 the Englunds were in Saudi Arabia. Even to mention the name Jesus was forbidden there, but Christian employees of the oil company had been allowed to form a Protestant Fellowship and invite ministers to conduct services. Englund enjoyed the fellowship and gladly shared the Word of God with them. The same month the Englunds visited Buraimi* where pioneer TEAM missionaries were making a brave attempt to establish a bridgehead in a Moslem stronghold. Even for such experienced travelers, flying in small planes over sandy wasteland and jolting along roadless desert was a new adventure. More was to follow. When asked to speak to the TEAM workers Englund had not expected that flies would outnumber people by a hundred-to-one. As morning by morning he preached from Paul's second letter to Timothy, he could never stop waving his hand in front of his mouth to keep out the persistent intruders.

With brief stops in Karachi** and Bangkok, the Englunds continued their travels by air until the familiar little island of Hong Kong came into view. As if by miracle, they were again with their beloved Chinese people. Among the first to welcome them was Katherine Tang who had so often been Englund's interpreter in the Bible School. When he accepted an invitation to preach in a camp crowded with refugees from the Mainland, he needed no interpreter. His Mandarin Chinese was easily understood.

Taiwan's welcome was exuberant and warm. Mrs. Su, widow of the Bible School principal, met them with affectionate greetings which eloquently expressed the feelings of many other Chinese friends. In making plans for Englund's visit, it had apparently been forgotten that he had already passed his eightieth year. The pace was fast and furious and filled with blessing. The first week was given to conferences on the premises of the Bible School which had been forced to close for lack of staff. Many graduates returned to hear their old and honored teacher expound the Scriptures once more. Some were discouraged and others had grown cold in heart, but as God's refreshing,

---

*Buraimi, an oasis in the Trucial Sheikdoms of the Arabian Peninsula.
**Karachi, a port city on the Arabian Sea and former capital of Pakistan.

mighty power flowed through Englund, every one of them dedicated his life to Christ anew.

Missionary conferences and special services in local churches crowded the rest of Englund's time in Taiwan. Congregations had grown during the seven years he had been absent and the lives of individuals evidenced that his work in the Lord had not been in vain. Mrs. Liu was an example. She had been converted through the ministry of Englund during a revival in Hupeh 48 years earlier. She married an evangelist who had been much blessed at the same time and together they faithfully served the Lord. When war and revolution unexpectedly brought Mr. and Mrs. Liu and the Englunds together in Taiwan years later, the evangelist was so delighted that he hugged William as if he would never let him go. On their final visit to Taiwan, the Englunds once more met Mrs. Liu, now a widow, but still actively serving Christ.

Japan was the final stop on their world tour. More than 150 TEAM missionaries were furthering the gospel there by preaching, radio, television, literature, camps, student centers and other means. Pastor Sukigara, with whom Englund had worked closely, had gone to be with Christ, but a steady stream of well-trained pastors, evangelists, and specialists in the fields of music, radio, literature and correspondence courses was coming from the Tokyo Christian College, and churches were slowly developing.

For the second time the Englunds crossed the Pacific by air, landing at Seattle on December 12, 1964. With fourteen stopovers, some lasting more than a week, they had circled the globe in 96 days. Compared with the 1940 trip from Shanghai to Sian which had taken 58 days it was a veritable modern travel miracle.

Trinity College and Trinity Evangelical Divinity School wrote to inform William Englund that they would be pleased to honor him with the degree of Doctor of Letters. Distinction is sometimes made between a degree *earned* through years of study in college or seminary and a degree commonly referred to as *honorary*, but when Englund bowed his head to have a doctor's hood placed on his shoulders he was receiving recognition for a lifetime of diligent study and intensive work.

He had never attended seminary, but was equally at ease in preaching Norwegian, Swedish, English and Chinese, basing exposition of the New Testament on a close familiarity with the Greek text. He did not have the opportunity to attend Bible school, but taught by the Holy Spirit he had fully qualified as principal and instructor of the Sian Bible Institute. In writing a Chinese commentary on the Pentateuch he had accomplished a monumental task. A worn out dictionary was silent testimony to years of patient labor. The *honorary* degree was not *unearned*. The audience with long and loud applause recognized that the honor was well deserved. William Englund smiled back at them, not hearing a sound. As the college President, Dr. Harry Evans, said afterward, "It is Trinity College that was honored that day."

21

The Sound of Trumpets

William Englund stood silently at his mother's place of prayer outside the old homestead near St. Hilaire on Red Lake River, Minnesota. The wind, blowing softly, rustled fallen leaves and revived memories. In a borrowed hut on March 17, 1882, without the elaborate facilities of a hospital, the skilled assistance of doctor or nurse, or even practical help from a country midwife, Ida Englund had safely given birth to her fourth child, William Gideon. The roof of the hut was thatched, the walls were unplastered boards of single thickness and there was a bare dirt floor. Before the baby was many months old he faced the first of many dangers to threaten his life.

A rampaging typhoid epidemic struck down Gustav and Ida Englund and their eldest son, Isadore. As William himself would experience years later in China, pioneers in Minnesota either trusted God for healing or died a lonely death. Doctors were almost unknown. Gustav and Ida recovered, but Isadore grew steadily worse. A doctor was finally found, but gave no hope for the dying boy. However, the parents, who had been converted during a great revival in their birthplace on Finland's Aland Island, knew the power of God. Praying silently, Ida looked at the fevered child, his throat so sore that he could not swallow. In faith she took a spoonful of water. "Just try once more and see if you can get it down," she whispered gently. She saw a tiny miracle as the cool water soothed his inflamed throat and was painfully swallowed. A greater miracle followed. Isadore recovered and lived to be a testimony to the lovingkindness of God. All his hair came out during the high fever. When it grew again it was wavy, distinguishing him from all other members of the family and making him the envy of his sisters.

Still weak from their illness, the Englunds were alarmed when they smelled smoke. Rushing from their log cabin, they were horrified to see the straw roof on fire from an overheated stovepipe. Gustav climbed unsteadily to the roof while Ida struggled part way up the ladder to pass buckets of water from her boys to her husband. But the little house could not be saved and in desperation the family salvaged their few belongings before flames destroyed their first home. Little William, wrapped in a quilt, was tenderly laid in a snowdrift.

Many years had passed but the old trees that enclosed Ida Englund's trysting place were still there. Into this sanctuary she had come often, feeling her sons were drifting away from God. She and Gustav had faithfully taken their children to church but its ritual left them cold. William's first reader had been a big Swedish Bible and she had been his first teacher, but a new, exciting world was drawing her children away from her and her God. She looked up and prayed, "Lord, if Thou wilt not soon come into our house and save our boys and reveal Thy reviving power, then the burden will become so heavy that I cannot live." Revival had come, beginning in Ida Englund.

A traveling preacher and a musician were holding evangelistic services in a rented hall in Thief River Falls. The singer's enthusiasm was so unrestrained that one evening he broke the strings of his guitar, but sang on undaunted. Crowds flocked to the services. "We cannot take all the boys. Some must stay to look after the stock. How will it be if we take William the first time and the others later?" suggested Gustav as he hitched the horse to the wagon for the eight mile trip.

William Englund could remember it all as if it were yesterday. The hall was crowded. When the evangelist began to speak, he felt a strange stirring in his heart, frightening and yet comforting, the kind of feeling he had when his father's strong voice called him for what might be either a warm supper or a scolding for coming home late. He wondered if he should raise his hand as others were doing. Before he had made up his mind, a man moved over to help but smelled so strongly of tobacco that he was repelled. His mother's attempts to talk with him on the way home failed and he was glad that the clip-clop of the horse's hoofs smothered the sound of his sobs.

Englund could remember, too, the evening when his brother Charles had been asked to read Psalm 103 as the family sat around the supper table. When Charles had come to the words, "Who forgiveth all thine iniquities," he had repeated them over and over again as if he could not escape their power. "Whose iniquities?," his mother had quietly asked, "and how many?" A great light had shone into Charles' soul. William had thought about it on his way home from a neighbor's house. He wondered if he were a Christian or not. As long as he could remember, he had been exposed to the love of

Christ, the sound of prayer and Scripture reading. In a vague and childish manner he had always believed in God, but the relationship was uncertain and indefinite. There was only one way to settle it. By the roadside, with a snowdrift as a prayer stool, he had knelt to ask Jesus Christ to forgive his sins and to live in him by His Spirit. The following week Ida's heart had nearly burst with joy as she heard her three sons pray aloud, one by one, at a cottage meeting in a neighbor's home. The miracle for which she had prayed had come to her family.

It was not long afterwards that Englund became sure of God's call to full time service. Pasturing the cattle gave him plenty of time for studying his Swedish pocket Bible. He would never forget the day when the Word of God was like a fire within him. The impulse to preach could not be repressed and there was no one in sight. He looked at the cattle, wandering leisurely towards the cool shelter of a grove of trees. They reminded him so much of honest, hard working farmers and their wives walking sedately to the house of God on the Sabbath that Englund laughed aloud. They would make a good congregation. He jumped up on an old tree stump, opened his Bible, announced the text and preached vigorously to his patient audience. Listening quietly to the impassioned preacher, the cattle made no visible response except to continue chewing their cuds as thoroughly as Englund himself would digest and redigest God's Word through many years.

All that was long ago. As Englund lingered on, reluctant to leave his mother's place of prayer, he thought of his father, a strong, stocky blue-eyed Swede. Gustav was a practical man with a strong sense of humor and vague ideas of American geography. In relating incidents he always concluded that "It took place in Pennsylvania" which, however, he could never find on a map. When William became 14, Gustav figured that his boy had enough learning to get through life. He put him to work on the farm, but that was not the only plan he had for his son. When he started a Sunday school in the little red schoolhouse, William was appointed teacher of the younger children. Manuals, flannelgraph material, handcraft lessons, and teacher's aids were things of the future, and William's best and only help came through prayer, diligent study of the Scriptures, and reliance on the Holy Spirit. God was preparing a principal and teacher for the Sian Bible Institute.

As he looked back over the years, Englund saw the crystal clear pattern of God's guidance. Pastor Johannesen, a Norwegian student in one of Fredrik Franson's seminars for possible missionary candidates, had developed into a Bible teacher. He arranged a short term Bible school in Teien Lutheran church, about 100 miles from the Englund home. William attended, gaining both a working knowledge of Norwegian and new understanding of God's Word. His eyes were also opened to the vital importance of systematic teaching of new Christians. At the same time he was being drawn unconsciously towards The Evangelical Alliance Mission and its founder Fredrik Franson.

He remembered his first sermon, preached when he was only 16 to a congregation meeting in his own home. His father had become the recognized spiritual leader of the community, and before long William became an assistant evangelist, often called to help in "special meetings." Among the first to accept Christ through his preaching was one of his former school teachers. To his own guitar accompaniment, William and his sister Olga had sung at a watch night service, and after hearing the message, the teacher had been converted. She never failed to correspond with Englund all his years in China.

But Minnesota winters, long, hard and a foretaste of bitter days in North China, took their toll among the Englund family members. Constant travel through snow and ice for preaching appointments weakened Englund's lungs and brought on tuberculosis. Deciding to move, on a spring day in 1902, the family boarded a train for the West. The crowd at the station to bid them farewell included many converts saved through William's ministry.

As the train began to move, a girl came running, calling out, "Please pray for me!" Englund recognized her as the daughter of a family with no interest in anything spiritual. The girl had attended meetings in the Englund home without making a decision. Years later, when he came home from his first term in China and was visiting in Minnesota, Englund learned that the girl had actually accepted Christ as she ran towards the moving train. The first time she confessed her faith, her younger sister also believed. She began visiting new settlers, gathering children around her for Bible study, holding informal meetings in homes and saw many come to Christ.

Seattle had been the next home for the family. William remembered the unexpected blessing of spending a few months in the old familiar house when he and Anna returned from China in 1939. It had been like reliving the days when he was a traveling evangelist, a satchel of clothes and Bible in one hand, and a guitar in the other. In those youthful years he had not realized that God was preparing him for an itinerant ministry in China, Hong Kong, Taiwan, North America, Europe and other parts of the world. The unfolding plan of God had never been as plain as the unfolded plan seen in retrospect.

Only once had there been a diversion from the main track of God's leading. From the time the family arrived in Seattle, Englund had depended on God alone to meet his financial needs through the generosity of God's people. But a Christian furniture dealer invited Englund to work for him, promising that all Sundays, and, if necessary, occasional weekdays, would be free for his preaching engagements.

If the arrangement proved satisfactory, then Englund would be made a partner in the business. The offer was accepted, but Englund soon found that he neither had wholehearted interest in furniture, nor time enough for increased opportunities in evangelism. Englund resigned to give all his time to the Lord's service and his employer accepted the decision sympathetically.

How had China come on his horizon? Englund clearly remembered Rev. Solomon Bergstrom whom God had led to Thief River Falls soon after an Evangelical Free Church had been started. Bergstrom, as energetic on furlough as in China, had thrown himself enthusiastically into the work and under his leadership a building had been erected. Englund's heart had warmed towards him at their first meeting and they were soon working together in campaigns. When Englund listened time after time to Bergstrom pleading for help in China, he was uncomfortably stirred, but lungs weakened by tuberculosis were an impossible handicap.

Englund chuckled as he thought of it. After more than 60 years of preaching his lungs were as good as ever, better in fact than when he had begun his ministry in Seattle. God had not failed. His mother's prayers had been answered above all she had asked or thought. His brother Charles, blessedly stuck at the third verse of Psalm 103, was now reunited with his parents and three other brothers in the presence of Christ. William himself had conducted Charles' funeral. Of the five sons he alone remained on earth. What rejoicing there would be when Gustav and Ida gathered all their children around them in the Heavenly courts to join in songs of praise. Would a guitar accompaniment be appropriate?

For the last time, William Englund walked slowly away from his mother's place of prayer. The swaying wind in the trees seemed to be gently consoling his spirit as he recalled the words of a song which he had composed one day in China when the going was hard:

> Mounting barrow for the road,
> Plodding on through heat and cold,
> Splashing through the mud and rain,
> Aching limbs and weary brain;
>> Do it all for Jesus,
>> He is coming soon.
> Bearing burdens not your own,
> Grieving over every wrong,
> Comforting the lone and sad,
> Loving all, both good and bad,
> Living often quite alone,
> Dreaming of your distant home,
> Feeling homesick many a while,
> Longing for a friendly smile.
> Thirsting for revival shower,

Pleading for the Spirit's power,
Watching for the coming dawn,
Waiting for the Lord's return.
Do it all for Jesus,
He is coming soon.

It was time to get back to Chicago. Englund had not forgotten that at the sendoff on their world tour, Dr. Mortenson had said, "We're praying that Brother Englund will get all the way to Revelation before he lays down his pen." Home once more in his little room, he opened his Chinese Bible to continue work on the commentary. The completed sections had clear outlines and practical exposition for the instruction of Chinese believers, and to assist them in teaching others. Notes on the first book of Samuel were not finished and never would be. His head was so very tired. Not many men of 86 would even consider so gigantic a task as a Bible commentary in Chinese and the Lord gently explained to His old and reliable servant that the time had come to take a rest.

One more year remained, tranquil and blessed. Private devotions which took him into the secret place of the Most High and intercessions which took him around the world filled much of his day. His family surrounded him with loving care. His daughter Winifred continued to enjoy the fragrance of his holy life. "Dad enriched our lives to the very end. We're grateful for every memory of him," she wrote in one of her books. The grandchildren felt the same. They would never forget his wonderful stories from the Bible and his songs in Chinese and English . . . and away in China, a veteran missionary would never forget either. As a little boy, Julius Bergstrom had been fascinated by Englund's talk to missionary children. "WATCH" had been written on a blackboard in large letters, and then followed the lesson to watch your Words, Actions, Temper, Character and Heart. Little Chinese children attracted by his gentleness and humor were his loyal friends in their adult years. In fact, children everywhere enjoyed his company. Sitting up in bed, William Englund called two of his granddaughters to his side. Like a patriarch of old he turned tenderly to them. "Well now, children," he said earnestly, "remember to live wholly for the Lord because Satan's ways are very subtle."

Englund never lost a keen awareness of evil powers relentlessly striving to keep men from the immeasurable riches in Christ. As long as he had breath, his passion was to lead people to a personal knowledge of the Savior. When a member of his wife's Bible class visited him, he smiled a welcome. He had not met her before, and after a few words of greeting, he unconsciously began talking in Chinese. Propped up by pillows, he energetically exhorted her to trust in Christ. Anna, sitting by his side, interpreted.

William rested in his little sanctuary, comfortable and at peace. His wife and daughter were quick to anticipate his needs. As he ap-

145

proached the "valley of the shadow," others came to help. First three nurses from Emmaus Bible School, and then Mrs. Harold Salveson, an old friend from Salem church, volunteered for duty by day or night. Familiar objects in the room turned his thoughts to China so often that when he spoke it was usually in Chinese, with an occasional lapse into Norwegian. He became less sure of where he was and uncertain of being awake or dreaming. Two visitors seemed vaguely familiar and he began chatting happily in Chinese with George Martin who had served with TEAM in Japan. But suddenly full clarity returned and with delight he recognized Vernon Mortenson who had been welcomed to Shensi as a young missionary in 1939. What wonderful times they had enjoyed together! Now he could talk with someone who would easily understand his Lantien accent. It never occurred to him to use English. Time stood on the threshold of eternity as the two men from TEAM headquarters committed their beloved brother to the Good Shepherd who was waiting to walk through the dark valley with His sheep, and make it light.

The time of prayer ended, Englund sank back in his bed, resting quietly in God. Past and present melted into one. People came and went, but whether they were real or memories, he could not be sure. Why didn't Pastor Chiang or Kuo Ming-yueh come to visit him? But they are with the Lord, which is far better. And that ragged, one-eyed Christian brother with his steel triangle and iron nail; what was it he sang? "Bringing in the sheaves" — surely he brought in many. What happened to him? He would find out one day. The blind man, drenched with sweat, staggering in with his daughter on his back — what an answer to prayer that was! Surely he's in the Father's house by now with sight restored. But the students must be waiting for the next lecture on Romans and Katherine Tang ready to interpret. No, that was Hong Kong, and this is Taiwan. Dear Brother Su Liang-i speaks in chapel today. How about giving that message on "Open eyes and burning hearts" tomorrow? Revival is always needed. How God had blessed that word in Japan — crowded Japan. He'd better phone Brother Sukigara to explain that he felt a little tired and might not be able to lecture today. And Anna — where is Anna, "Queen of Englund?" He felt her hand, and knew that she was beside him as she had always been. God had brought them through so much together; war, famine, sickness, and trials innumerable. Anna who had so often made a home for him, lovingly welcomed him back after many a journey, shared the hardships of travel, faced their common dangers, and carried full responsibility when he was away, Anna was still with him. And Winifred, too. How wonderfully God had preserved the family, binding them together in His eternal love.

But what had happened to his fellow missionaries? It was time for the Field Council. Perhaps they had been delayed along the way. Those mules could be stubborn creatures, especially in mud. Recent rains had been heavy, like the showers of revival blessing. Maybe bandits were the problem. T. J. Bach hadn't written lately, even though the accounts were overdue. That was because of so many special meetings in dear old Lantien . . . but Bach was with Christ. So many were there, warriors of Jesus Christ, singing the song of the Lamb that was slain, and giving loud praise to God. He seemed to hear music, triumphant and strong like the opening bars of a stirring symphony . . . and then singing, swelling in volume and very clear. Could it be that his deaf ears were open at last? It was so indeed. Praise God for evermore! "And all the trumpets sounded for him on the other side."